The Bull, the Bear and the Planets

Trading the Financial Markets Using Astrology

M. G. Bucholtz, B.Sc., MBA

iUniverse, Inc.
Bloomington

The Bull, the Bear and the Planets
Trading the Financial Markets Using Astrology

iUniverse books may be ordered through booksellers or by contacting:

iUniverse
1663 Liberty Drive
Bloomington, IN 47403
www.iuniverse.com
1-800-Authors (1-800-288-4677)

ISBN: 978-1-4759-8002-8 (sc)
ISBN: 978-1-4759-8004-2 (hc)
ISBN: 978-1-4759-8003-5 (ebk)

Library of Congress Control Number: 2013904065

Printed in the United States of America

iUniverse rev. date: 03/07/2013

Disclaimer

All material provided herein is based on financial market observations of the author and material gleaned from astrological publications researched by the author to supplement his own trading. This book is written with sincere intent for those who actively trade and invest in the financial markets and who are looking to incorporate astrological phenomena into their market activity. While the material presented herein has proven reliable to the author in his personal trading and investing activity, there is no guarantee the material herein will continue to be reliable into the future. The author and publisher assume no liability whatsoever for any investment or trading decisions made by readers of this book. The reader alone is responsible for all trading and investment outcomes and is further advised not to exceed his or her risk tolerances when trading or investing on the financial markets.

Acknowledgements

To my beautiful wife Jeanne, who continues to inspire me in so many ways and without whose encouragement this book would not have been possible.

Contents

Figures and Tables

Introduction

Call me a rebel. Call me a radical. I have never been one to resign myself to mainstream thinking. In 2002, when I decided to become an Investment Advisor, I joined a small investment firm in western Canada that had a reputation for thinking outside the box. I was mentored by two seasoned Investment Advisors who deepened my understanding of technical chart analysis. I learned that markets shift from being in an uptrend to being in a downtrend and back again across both short and longer time horizons. I learned that if I followed these trend changes using technical chart analysis I would be in tune with the rhythm of the markets. This refreshing approach represented a clear break from the academic financial theory espoused as part of the exam regimen required for the licensing process with the Investment Dealers Association of Canada. And thus began my quest to delve into the uncanny and esoteric forces that align with trend changes in the financial markets.

In 2003, after a series of reflective discussions with a fellow Investment Advisor, I applied to join a local Masonic Lodge. Early on in my Masonic education, I was urged to contemplate the hidden mysteries of science and nature through further study of the harmony between arithmetic, geometry and astronomy. Nature comprises the whole of our material universe from the solar system all the way to the smallest measurable particle of matter. Science is the disciplined use of mathematics to describe the material universe in terms of prediction and control. The process of contemplating the mysteries of science and nature is what Masons call enlightenment. As I delved further into the relationship between science and nature, I learned the venerable market trader, W.D. Gann, had been a Mason as well. Gann spent much of his trading career pursuing the study of sacred math and astrological phenomena and applying it to trading the markets. Knowing that Gann had been a Mason piqued my curiosity and my journey to learn more about the forces that affect the financial markets took on an almost urgent tone. I began to devour literature related not only to the ideas of W.D. Gann but also to esoteric mathematical patterns of science and nature.

I soon learned, however, that my journey was to be a lonely one. Very few people in the financial industry are interested in contemplating the uncanny and esoteric patterns of science and nature, let alone astrological phenomena. In order to be accepted into the mainstream of the financial industry, one has to adhere rigidly to decades of econometric financial theory and modelling groupthink.

As financial market investing became mainstream in the 1920s, econometric modelling was introduced to explain market behaviour. The seminal work that opened the door to decades of such modelling came in 1934 when Graham and Dodd produced *Security Analysis* in which they advocated using intrinsic value as a tool that could help identify suitable investments. In 1938, John Burr Williams penned *The Theory of Investment Value* in which he introduced the notion of discounting future expected streams of dividend payments to better define intrinsic value. In 1959, Harry Markowitz focused on risk not being uniformly equal among stock market investments when he introduced Modern Portfolio Theory in *Portfolio Selection—Efficient Diversification of Investments*. William Sharpe extended this manner of thinking in 1970 with his work *Portfolio Theory and Capital Markets*. Fast forward to the present and one can easily find shelves of journals in university libraries, brimming with market theory.

Because econometric models and theories underpin mainstream thinking across the financial investment industry, they also form the backbone of entire programs of study leading to the MBA degree and the CFA (Chartered Financial Analyst) designation. While graduates of these programs may feel empowered and ready to take on the financial world, they do not realize they have largely consumed a concentrated diet of economic theory during their course of study.

In 2005, driven by curiosity, I embarked on the CFA journey but to no surprise quickly grew weary of the flaws I perceived in the theories being advanced to explain market movements. I found it difficult to embrace theories that purported to predict future stock prices based on enterprise value, earnings data or cash flow. I likewise found it hard to accept that complex credit default swaps and asset backed obligation instruments were being hailed as proper investment strategies complete with predictive models.

In 2008, the 'theoryland' crowd was given a long overdue wakeup call when financial markets around the globe convulsed and major indices plunged. Since then, the winds of change have started to blow. A 2012 *Financial Times* Special Report on MBA Education makes it clear that knowing the theory of business is no longer enough to get students where they want to be. In this same report, Peter Trufano, Dean of Oxford University's Said Business School, notes ". . . *post-recession and market crash, students need a deep understanding of the economy from a variety of perspectives. Science, technology and politics all play a role."* Canadian David Orell, author of the books *Truth or Beauty* and *Economyths* does an excellent job of assaulting mainstream economic thinking to provide his readers with a wake-up call. Orell's books are a reminder that our desire to cling to theory is part of a centuries-old impulse to see the world in simple, elegant terms.

Despite some hopeful signs of change and the hard work of authors like David Orell to painstakingly expose flaws in econometric models, I find it disheartening that the financial industry continues to cling to narrow theories when it is obvious that many of the causes of events in our world are intangible and cannot be seen, felt or heard. We know that tides at the seashore rise and fall. Try as we may, we can never see or feel the actual force that moves the water. We know that earthquakes and volcanos can cause tremendous damage. Yet, we are unable to see the shifting tectonic plates deep in the Earth's crust that cause these events. Scientists have now explained how the gravitational pulls of Jupiter and Saturn on the Sun's gaseous matter contribute to solar sunspot activity. Yet, we cannot readily feel their gravitational pulls. Because we are unable to physically see and feel the causes of events around us, we immediately opt for the comfort of eloquently penned explanatory theories derived from large streams of data collected over long spans of time. And so it is that individual investors entrusting their hard earned dollars to Investment Advisors and Financial Planners soon become resigned to the notion that investing in the financial markets is a weary, mind numbing, long term process overlain and interwoven with models, analyst opinions and theory.

It need not be so.

The financial markets are nothing more than one big psychological event ruled by the emotions of fear and hope. When market participants are fearful, they sell. When they are feeling hopeful, they buy. If intangible forces are capable of causing events like tidal motion, earthquakes, volcanos and sunspots, surely then it must be plausible that these same forces can influence the emotions of fear and hope within human beings and thereby influence buying and selling activity on the markets.

Science tells us planet Earth is one gigantic electromagnet with poles situated north and south. The various other planets that comprise our solar system are also electromagnetic in nature and exert gravitational pulls on each other as well as on planet Earth. Science also tells us the Sun shines on our gigantic electromagnet while continually emitting high frequency waves of radiation.

In grade school science class we all at one point played with a simple prism. We learned that by varying the angle of light being shone on the prism, we could influence the refraction of the light to produce different colors. And so it is with the Sun's radiated energy experienced by mankind on the surface of the Earth. As the various planets orbit the Sun and make different angles with one another, the intensity of the Sun's radiation reflecting off their surfaces varies. As a result, the intensity of the Sun's radiation reaching Earth varies. This reasoning forms the basis for the notion that our emotions are continually changing in response to these variances. By extension of the argument, it is these changing emotions that can influence the behavior of our buying and selling patterns as we trade on the financial markets.

As a result of my trading experiences on the markets and my esoteric research over the past decade, I have now largely divorced myself from the theories that continue to be embraced by the financial investment industry. Trading and investing have become vibrant and exciting for me. I have come to embrace astrological phenomena such as Moon phases, planetary aspects and synodic patterns. I use these phenomena and patterns in close conjunction with technical chart analysis techniques to look for trend change developments on indices, ETFs, individual stocks and commodity futures.

For the record, I do not consider myself to be an astrologer. I use astrology only to trade the markets. I do not use astrology to counsel people or predict individual fates. My educational background includes an Engineering degree from Queen's University in Canada and an MBA from Heriot Watt University in Scotland. As a result of my engineering bent and my Masonic contemplations, I derive great satisfaction from observing patterns of astrology—especially those that align with the financial markets. The science behind how and why astrologic patterns often align with the trend changes of the markets is deep, mysterious and elusive. These characteristics further add to the satisfaction I derive when applying astrology to the markets.

The decision to write this book was a struggle. For quite some time I debated whether or not to even share this material with others given the skeptical looks and comments I receive when trying to explain to close associates that science and nature play a role in the behavior of financial markets. The turning point for me came in early 2012 when I attended the United Astrology Conference in New Orleans, USA where an entire curriculum track was devoted to financial astrology. Listening to the discussions in the hallways between lectures, I realized I was not alone in embracing intangible forces that move the markets. There are ever-growing numbers of traders and investors who are openly embracing the connection between financial market behavior and the intangible forces of the cosmos.

This book introduces the reader to correlations between planetary cycles, planetary aspects, lunar phenomena and the markets. These correlations are not new. In fact, they have been known about and used successfully by traders and investors for many decades. There have been many colorful personalities over the years aside from just W.D. Gann who have employed astrology towards successful trading. In fact, some of the oldest manuscripts researched while preparing this book date back to the early 1900s. Indeed, the most enjoyable part of researching and writing this book was discovering and reading historical financial astrology books and papers found in various libraries across North America.

The correlations you will learn about in this book should never be blindly used in a vacuum. Rather, astrology should always be used in conjunction with technical chart analysis and with the prevailing short and longer term trends of the markets. Ideally to derive maximum satisfaction from this book, you should have a comfortable grasp on the commonly used technical chart analysis techniques. As well, you should also have copies of Ephemeris Tables spanning 1900-2000 and 2000 forward. I personally use the *New American Ephemeris for the 21st Century* and its counterpart *New American Ephemeris for the 20th Century* which are readily available at most bookstores. Alternatively, you may also consider getting an astrology software program that will provide you with the same data.

After reading this book and applying some of the astrological concepts presented in it, I have no doubt you will come to view our universe in a very different, almost reverent way. I expect many of you will even seek to further your knowledge of astrology through in depth study. I hope your trading and investing activity will take on a new personal meaning as you come to view the financial markets in a different way.

CHAPTER ONE

Astrology Basics for the Market Trader

Astrology is an ancient science that describes the influence of the planets on events of nature and behaviour of mankind. This ancient science is rooted in thousands of years of observation across many civilizations.

- The ancient Sumerians, Akkadians and Babylonians between the 4th and 2nd centuries BC believed the affairs of mankind could be gauged by watching the motions of the stars and planets. They recorded their predictions and future indications of prosperity and calamity on clay tablets. These early recordings form the very foundations of modern day astrology.
- Ancient Egyptian artifacts show that high priests Petosiris and Necepso who lived during the reign of Ramses II were revered for their knowledge of astrology. The Egyptian culture is also thought to have developed a 12 month x 30 day recordation method for time based on the repeated appearances of constellations.
- Ancient Indian and Chinese artifacts reveal that astrology has held an esteemed place in those societies for many thousands of years.
- Hipparchus, Pythagoras and Plato are revered names from the Greek era. Historians think Pythagoras may have assigned mathematical values to the relations between celestial bodies and Plato may have offered up predictions relating celestial bodies to human fates. Hipparchus is thought to have compiled a star catalogue and in so doing was the first to popularize astrology.

- During Roman times, astrology and divination were used for political gain with important military figures surrounding themselves with seers and diviners. Ptolemy and Valens stand out from the time of the Roman Empire as writers on astrology. In 126 AD, Ptolemy penned four books on the influence of the stars which collectively are called the *Tetrabiblos*. In 160 AD, Valens penned *Anthologies* in which he further summarized the principles of astrology.

But, following the conversion of Emperor Constantine to Christianity, in 312 AD, divination and magic became a crime according to the Church and astrology began a slow retreat to the sidelines where for the most part it remains today. However, despite this sidelining by a Church seeking to protect its authority, astrology has been used in more modern history by leading thinkers such as Galilei Galileo, Tycho Brahe, Nostradamus, Johannes Kepler, Sir Francis Bacon, Isaac Newton and Benjamin Franklin. Indeed we owe much of our current state of scientific advancement to these brave souls who refused to let astrology fade away and become a distant memory.

The Zodiac

In our solar system, the Sun is at the center. The Earth, Moon, planets and various other asteroid bodies all collectively comprise our planetary system. The various planets and other asteroid bodies rotate the 360 degrees around the Sun following a path called the ecliptic plane. Picture a gigantic band that encircles the 360 degrees of the planetary system. Divide this band into twelve equal portions of 30 degrees each and the result is what astrologers call the *zodiac*. The twelve portions of the zodiac all have names including Aries, Cancer, Leo and so on. If these names sound familiar, they should. You routinely see all twelve names in the daily horoscope section of your morning newspaper. The starting point or zero degree point of the zodiac sign Aries is deemed to be at the Spring Equinox of each year as shown in Figure 1-1.

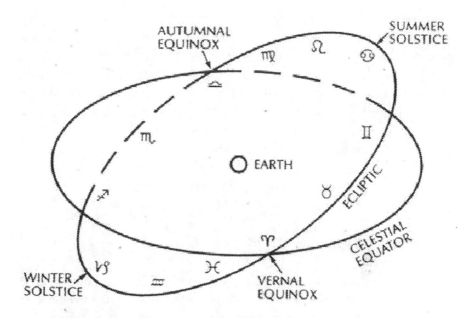

DIAGRAM OF ECLIPTIC AND CELESTIAL EQUATOR

Figure 1-1 The Ecliptic

Geocentric and Heliocentric Astrology

Astrology comes in two distinct varieties—*geocentric* and *heliocentric*. In *geocentric* astrology, the Earth is taken to be the vantage point for observing the planets as they pass through the signs of the zodiac. Owing to the different times for the various planets to each orbit the Sun, from an astrologer's vantage point on Earth, it appears as though from time to time certain planets make distinct angles (called *aspects*) with one another and also with the Sun. The *aspects* that are commonly used in astrology are 0, 30, 45, 60, 90, 120, 150 and 180 degrees.

In *heliocentric* astrology, the Sun is taken to be the vantage point and to an observer positioned on the Sun, it likewise appears as though various planets are making angles with other planets from time to time.

I use both types of astrology to compliment my trading activity, but I do find I am slowly developing a preference for the heliocentric variety. This may be because it is a bit cleaner than the geocentric method, for heliocentric astrology does not worry about features such as Ascendant, Descendant, MC and IC. Most of the examples you will see throughout this book are based on *geocentric* astrology, but you will also see how *heliocentric* astrology plays a role in trading the markets too, especially when it comes to commodity futures. After reading this book, I encourage you to take a look at both methods. Like me, you will probably find that you start to develop a preference for one method over the other.

Ascendant, Descendant, MC and IC

As the Earth rotates on its axis once in every 24 hours, an observer situated on Earth will detect an apparent motion of the zodiac. Astrologers further apply four cardinal points to the zodiac, almost like the north, south, east and west points on a compass. The east point is termed the *ascendant* and is often abbreviated Asc. The west point is termed the *descendant* and is often abbreviated Dsc. The south point is termed the *Mid-Heaven* (from the Latin *Medium Coeli*) and is often abbreviated MC. The north point is termed the *Imum Coeli* (Latin for bottom of the sky) and is abbreviated IC. These cardinal points are often used when applying astrology to the markets. For example, when the New York Stock Exchange officially opened for business on May 17, 1792, it had its ascendant in Cancer, its MC in Aries, its Descendant in Capricorn and its IC in Libra.

Mythology and Meanings

Throughout history, various stories and characteristic behaviours have been assigned to the 12 signs of the zodiac. The diagram in Figure 1-2 provides a visual rendering of the 12 signs and the traditional imagery that relates to each sign. What then follows is an amusing bit of mythology for each sign.

Figure 1-2 The Zodiac Signs

Aries (0 to 30 degrees, 21 March-20 April)

According to Greek mythology, Nephele, the mother of Phrixus and Helles, gave her sons a ram with a golden fleece. To escape their evil stepmother, Hera, the sons mounted the ram and fled. When they reached the sea, Helles fell into the water and perished. Phrixus survived the ordeal, the ram's fleece was dedicated to Zeus who then raised the ram into the heavens and made it a constellation.

Taurus (30 to 60 degrees, 21 April-21 May)

According to Roman legend, Jupiter took the form of a bull and became infatuated with the fair maiden Europa. When Europa decided to ride the bull, he rushed into the sea and whisked Europa off to Crete. Jupiter then raised the bull into the heavens where it became a star.

5

Gemini (60 to 90 degrees, 22 May-21 June)

In Greek mythology, the twins are considered to be Hercules and Apollo. In Roman legend, the twins are said to be Castor and Pollux, the twin sons of Leda. Pollux was the son of Zeus, who seduced Leda, while Castor was the son of Tyndareus, king of Sparta and Leda's husband. When Castor died, Pollux begged his father Zeus to give Castor immortality, and he did, by uniting them together in the heavens.

Cancer (90 to 120 degrees, 22 June-23 July)

Roman legend says that Cancer is the crab that bit Hercules during his fight with the Hydra and it was placed in the heavens as a star by Juno, the enemy of Hercules.

Leo (120 to 150 degrees, 24 July-23 August)

Legend says that Hercules battled with the Nemean lion and won. Zeus raised the lion to the heavens and made it into a star.

Virgo (150 to 180 degrees, 24 August-23 September)

Legend has it that Virgo is a constellation modelled after Justitia, daughter of Astraeus and Ancora, who lived before man sinned. After man sinned, Justitia returned to the heavens.

Libra (180 to 210 degrees, 24 September-23 October)

Libra was known in Babylonian astronomy as scales that were held sacred to the sun god Shamash, who was also the patron of truth and justice. In Roman mythology, Libra is considered to depict the scales held by Astraea, the goddess of justice.

Scorpio (210 to 240 degrees, 24 October-22 November)

According to Greek mythology, Orion boasted to Diana and Latona that he could kill every animal on Earth. So they sent for a scorpion which stung Orion to death. Jupiter then raised the scorpion to the heavens.

Sagittarius (240 to 270 degrees, 23 November-22 December)

In Babylonian legend, Sagittarius was the God of War. In Greek legend, Sagittarius is denoted as a centaur (half man, half horse) in the act of shooting an arrow. In Roman legend, Sagittarius was a centaur who killed himself when he accidently dropped one of Hercules' poisoned arrows on his hoof.

Capricorn (270 to 300 degrees, 23 December-20 January)

In Greek legend, during the war with the giants, the Greek Gods were driven into Egypt. In order to escape the wrath of the encroaching giants, each Greek God changed his shape. The God Pan leapt into the river Nile and turned the upper part of his body into a goat and the lower part into a fish, a combination deemed worthy by Jupiter who raised him to the heavens.

Aquarius (300 to 330 degrees, 21 January-19 February)

According to legend, Deucalion the son of Prometheus was raised to the heavens after surviving the great deluge that flooded the world.

Pisces (330 to 360 degrees, 20 February-20 March)

In Greek legend, Aphrodite and Eros were surprised by Typhon while playing along the river Nile. They jumped into the water and were changed into two fishes.

As we can see, astrology dates back many millennia. Ancient societies correlated their events and future activities to the planets. Modern society, however, has put astrology on the back burner. But, slowly, traders and investors are starting to accept it again.

Now, let's see how lunar astrology can be used as a tool to trade and invest in the markets.

CHAPTER TWO

Trading Using Lunar Astrology

Look skyward on any clear night and you will see the Moon in one of its various phases. The Moon is the closest of all the planetary bodies to the Earth and has long been held in fascination by mankind.

In traditional astrology, the Moon is associated with changing mood or health. In 6th century Constantinople (modern day Istanbul, Turkey), physicians at the court of Emperor Justinian advised that gout could be cured by inscribing verses of Homer on a copper plate when the Moon was in the sign of Libra or Leo. In 17th century France, astrologers used the Moon to explain mood changes in women. In 17th century England, herbal remedy practitioners advised people to pluck the petals of the peony flower when the Moon was waning. During the Renaissance period, it was thought that dreams could come true if the Moon was in the signs of Taurus, Leo, Aquarius or Scorpio.

In modern times, the Moon continues to be recognized as a powerful celestial body. And there exists a fascinating correlation between the Moon and financial market behaviour. My observations have shown that for selected stocks lunar phenomena when used in combination with technical chart analysis can add a whole new dimension to trading and investing. This chapter examines lunar phases and variations in the Moon's distance from Earth. These phenomena are closely related to short term changes of trend on stocks and commodity futures. This chapter also looks at the North Node of the Moon and its influence on markets as it changes signs of the zodiac. The scientific relation between lunar phenomena and the markets is elusive but if the gravitational pull of the Moon can influence tides, surely it also influences our emotions of fear and hope which in turn rule our investment buying and selling decisions.

Lunar Phases and the Synodic Month

The phases of the Moon are well-known in scientific circles for their effects on the ocean's tides and on the mating behaviour in certain species. The Full Moon is known to psychologists for bumping up the rates of violent crime and irrational behaviour. In fact, the terms *'lunacy'* and *'lunatic'* are drawn from the widespread observation of the way the Moon affects mental and emotional states. Many serious gardeners also know that the phases of the Moon affect suitable times for planting, fertilizing and harvesting.

Much like the planets orbit the Sun, the Moon orbits the Earth. The Moon orbits the 360 degrees around the Earth in a plane of motion called the lunar orbit plane. This orbit plane is inclined at about 5 degrees to the ecliptic plane of the Earth. The Moon orbits Earth with a slightly elliptical pattern in approximately 27.3 days, relative to an observer located on a fixed frame of reference-the Sun. This is known as a *sidereal month*. However to an observer located on Earth, during one sidereal month, the Earth has also revolved part way around the Sun, making the average apparent orbit time longer than the sidereal month at approximately 29.5 days. This 29.5 day period of time is known as a *synodic month* or more commonly a *lunar month*.

To an observer located on planet Earth, the Moon can be seen making various angles or phases to the Sun as the Earth journeys around the Sun. In fact, there are eight such phases of the Moon that astrologers work with. The New Moon occurs when the Moon is 0 degrees (or conjunct) to the Sun. The Crescent Phase occurs at a Sun-Moon angle of 45 degrees. The First Quarter Moon is at 90 degrees. The Gibbous Phase is at 135 degrees. The Full Moon is at 180 degrees. The Disseminating Phase is at 225 degrees. The Last Quarter Phase is at 270 degrees. The Balsamic Phase is at 315 degrees. For example, on February 25, 2012 the Sun, relative to an observer on Earth, was seen to be at a zodiac location of 6 degrees Pisces. The Moon was seen to be at 6 degrees of Virgo. This is a separation of 180 degrees and indeed February 25,2012 was the date of a Full Moon.

When considering the Moon in the context of the financial markets, the two most impactful phases are the New Moon (0 degrees to the Sun) and the Full Moon (180 degrees to the Sun). Eclipses are also very potent events for market traders to be alert to. The following diagram taken from *Business Astrology 101*, by Astrologer Georgia Stathis illustrates the various lunar phases.

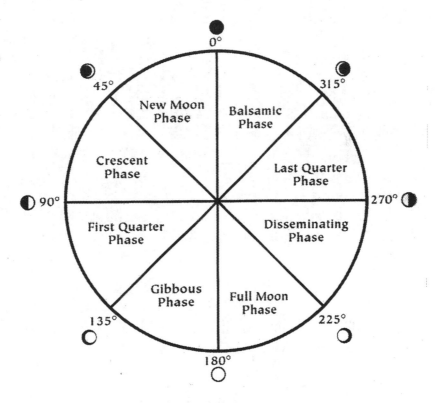

Figure 2-1 Lunar Phases

With an Ephemeris in hand one can easily track Moon phases for a given month. The illustration in Figure 2-2 depicts a page taken from the *New American Ephemeris for the 21st Century*. The arrow in the image points to the section of the page that provides Moon data for the month in question (December 2012). In this example, one can see the New Moon will occur on December 13 and the Full Moon will occur on December 28 which also happens to be an eclipse date.

December 2012 **LONGITUDE**

Day	Sid.Time	☉	0 hr ☽	Noon ☽	True ☊	☿	♀	♂	⚳	♃	♄	♅	♆	♇
1 Sa	4 41 01	9♐11 45	4♋59 00	10♋56 35	26♏03.6	19♏30.3	11♏04.6	10♑34.5	0♋40.4	11♊34.8	6♏37.1	4♈40.9	0♓28.2	8♑1
2 Su	4 44 58	10 12 33	16 55 46	22 56 50	26R 01.5	20 11.0	12 19.1	11 20.5	0R 28.7	11R 26.7	6 43.6	4R 40.3	0 28.9	8
3 M	4 48 54	11 13 23	29 00 10	5♌06 06	25 59.1	20 58.4	13 33.7	12 06.6	0 16.8	11 18.5	6 50.0	4 39.7	0 29.6	8
4 Tu	4 52 51	12 14 14	11♌15 03	17 27 24	25 56.9	21 51.5	14 48.3	12 52.8	0 04.7	11 10.3	6 56.4	4 39.2	0 30.4	8
5 W	4 56 47	13 15 07	23 43 33	0♍03 58	25 55.1	22 49.8	16 02.9	13 38.9	29♊52.3	11 02.1	7 02.7	4 38.7	0 31.2	8
6 Th	5 00 44	14 16 00	6♍29 04	12 59 14	25D 54.1	23 52.5	17 17.5	14 25.2	29 39.6	10 54.0	7 09.0	4 38.3	0 32.0	8
7 F	5 04 41	15 16 55	19 34 53	26 16 21	25 53.9	24 59.0	18 32.2	15 11.5	29 26.8	10 45.8	7 15.3	4 37.9	0 32.9	8
8 Sa	5 08 37	16 17 52	3♎03 55	9♎57 47	25 54.6	26 08.9	19 46.9	15 57.8	29 13.7	10 37.7	7 21.5	4 37.6	0 33.7	8
9 Su	5 12 34	17 18 49	16 58 04	24 04 42	25 56.0	27 21.7	21 01.6	16 44.2	29 00.5	10 29.6	7 27.6	4 37.4	0 34.7	8
10 M	5 16 30	18 19 48	1♏17 32	8♏36 13	25 57.4	28 37.0	22 16.4	17 30.6	28 47.0	10 21.6	7 33.7	4 37.2	0 35.6	8
11 Tu	5 20 27	19 20 48	16 00 15	23 28 54	25R 58.5	29 54.5	23 31.2	18 17.0	28 33.4	10 13.5	7 39.8	4 37.0	0 36.6	8
12 W	5 24 23	20 21 49	1♐01 19	8♐36 27	25 58.7	1♐13.9	24 46.0	19 03.5	28 19.7	10 05.6	7 45.8	4 36.9	0 37.6	8
13 Th	5 28 20	21 22 51	16 13 10	23 50 11	25 57.6	2 34.8	26 00.8	19 50.1	28 05.8	9 57.7	7 51.7	4D 36.8	0 38.7	8
14 F	5 32 16	22 23 54	1♑26 15	9♑00 05	25 55.1	3 57.2	27 15.7	20 36.7	27 51.9	9 49.9	7 57.6	4 36.8	0 39.8	8
15 Sa	5 36 13	23 24 57	16 30 29	23 56 21	25 51.5	5 20.8	28 30.6	21 23.3	27 37.8	9 42.1	8 03.4	4 36.9	0 40.9	8
16 Su	5 40 10	24 26 02	1♒16 45	8♒30 58	25 47.2	6 45.5	29 45.5	22 10.0	27 23.7	9 34.4	8 09.2	4 37.0	0 42.0	8
17 M	5 44 06	25 27 06	15 38 25	22 38 47	25 43.0	8 11.0	1♐00.4	22 56.7	27 09.5	9 26.8	8 14.9	4 37.1	0 43.2	8
18 Tu	5 48 03	26 28 11	29 31 52	6♓17 44	25 39.3	9 37.4	2 15.3	23 43.4	26 55.3	9 19.3	8 20.6	4 37.4	0 44.4	8
19 W	5 51 59	27 29 16	12♓56 32	19 28 36	25 36.9	11 04.5	3 30.3	24 30.2	26 41.1	9 11.9	8 26.2	4 37.6	0 45.6	8
20 Th	5 55 56	28 30 22	25 54 19	2♈14 13	25D 35.9	12 32.2	4 45.2	25 17.0	26 26.9	9 04.6	8 31.7	4 37.9	0 46.9	8
21 F	5 59 52	29 31 27	8♈28 49	14 38 43	25 36.2	14 00.5	6 00.2	26 03.8	26 12.7	8 57.4	8 37.1	4 38.3	0 48.2	8
22 Sa	6 03 49	0♑32 33	20 44 32	26 46 53	25 37.6	15 29.3	7 15.2	26 50.7	25 58.5	8 50.3	8 42.5	4 38.7	0 49.5	8
23 Su	6 07 45	1 33 40	2♉46 21	8♉43 32	25 39.4	16 58.5	8 30.1	27 37.5	25 44.4	8 4	8 47.9	4 39.2	0 50.9	9
24 M	6 11 42	2 34 46	14 39 00	20 33 15	25R 41.0	18 28.2	9 45.2	28 24.5	25 30.4	8 3	8 53.1	4 39.7	0 52.2	9
25 Tu	6 15 39	3 35 53	26 26 48	2♊20 06	25 41.6	19 58.3	11 00.2	29 11.4	25 16.5	8 2	8 58.3	4 40.2	0 53.7	9
26 W	6 19 35	4 36 59	8♊13 32	14 07 30	25 40.6	21 28.7	12 15.2	29 58.4	25 02.6	8 2	9 03.4	4 40.9	0 55.1	9
27 Th	6 23 32	5 38 07	20 02 18	25 58 14	25 37.7	22 59.5	13 30.3	0♒45.4	24 48.9	8 1	9 08.5	4 41.5	0 56.6	9
28 F	6 27 28	6 39 14	1♋55 33	7♋54 27	25 32.7	24 30.6	14 45.3	1 32.4	24 35.4	8	13.5	4 42.3	0 58.0	9
29 Sa	6 31 25	7 40 21	13 55 08	19 57 47	25 25.9	26 02.0	16 00.4	2 19.5	24 22.0	8	18.4	4 43.0	0 59.6	9
30 Su	6 35 21	8 41 29	26 02 32	2♌09 32	25 17.8	27 33.8	17 15.5	3 06.5	24 08.7	7 5	9 23.2	4 43.9	1 01.1	9
31 M	6 39 18	9 42 37	8♌18 55	14 30 50	25 09.1	29 05.9	18 30.6	3 53.6	23 55.7	7 52	9 28.0	4 44.7	1 02.7	9

Astro Data	Planet Ingress	Last Aspect	☽ Ingress	Last Aspect	☽ Ingress	☽ Phases & Eclipses	Astro Data
Dy Hr Mn	Dy Hr Mn	Dy Hr Mn	Dy Hr Mn	Dy Hr Mn	Dy Hr Mn	Dy Hr Mn	1 November 2012
☿ R 6 23:05	☿ ♏R 14 7:43	2 9:23 ♂ ☍	♋ 3 7:44	2 6:56 ☿ △	♌ 3 1:58	7 0:37 ☾ 15♌00	Julian Day # 41213
☽0S 9 13:56	♂ ♑ 17 2:37	4 8:38 ☉ △	♌ 5 19:40	4 22:09 ☿ □	♍ 5 11:53	13 22:09 ● 21♏57	SVP 5♓04'37"
♆ D 11 7:53	☉ ♐ 21 21:51	7 15:28 ♂ △	♍ 8 4:36	7 10:37 ☿ ⚹	♎ 7 18:36	13 22:12:55 • T 04'02"	GC 27♐01.1 ⚵ 23♓51.3
♄⚻♅ 16 0:28	♀ ♏ 22 1:21	10 0:28 ♂ □	♎ 10 9:36	9 0:38 ☉ ⚹	♏ 9 21:52	20 14:33 ☽ 28♒41	Eris 22♈00.0R ⚴ 13♐10.7
☽0N 22 3:25		12 5:14 ♂ ⚹	♏ 12 11:11	11 13:09 ♀ ☌	♐ 11 22:23	28 14:47 ○ 6♊47	⚷ 5♓04.5R ⚶ 25♊09.1
☿ D 26 22:51	⚳ ♊R 4 9:07	14 10:40 ☿ ☌	♐ 14 10:53	13 8:43 ☉ ☌	♑ 13 21:44	28 14:34 • A 0.915	☽ Mean ☊ 26♏49.6
	☿ ♐ 11 1:41	16 9:45 ♂ ☌	♑ 16 10:37	15 21:16 ♀ ⚹	♒ 15 21:54		
☽0S 6 22:22	♀ ♐ 16 4:39	18 5:55 ☉ ⚹	♒ 18 12:11	17 18:13 ☉ ⚹	♓ 18 0:49	6 15:33 ☾ 14♍55	1 December 2012
♅ D 13 12:03	☉ ♑ 21 11:13	20 14:33 ☉ □	♓ 20 16:56	20 5:20 ☉ □	♈ 20 7:44	13 8:43 ● 21♐45	Julian Day # 41243
☽0N 19 10:47	♂ ♒ 26 0:50	22 6:33 ☿ △	♈ 23 1:13	22 12:58 ♂ □	♉ 22 18:26	20 5:20 ☽ 28♓44	SVP 5♓04'32"
♃⚻♇ 21 3:37	☿ ♑ 31 14:04	24 1:36 ♃ ⚹	♉ 25 12:19	25 5:59 ♂ △	♊ 25 7:14	28 10:22 ○ 7♋06	GC 27♐01.2 ⚵ 22♓46.2
♃⚻♄ 22 15:04		27 0:58 ☿ ☍	♊ 28 0:59	27 6:51 ☿ ☍	♋ 27 20:08		Eris 21♈45.1R ⚴ 23♐27.9
♄⚹♇ 27 1:42		29 1:05 ♃ ☌	♋ 30 13:56	28 14:44 ♄ △	♌ 30 7:46		⚷ 5♓06.5 ⚶ 19♊49.2
							☽ Mean ☊ 25♏14.3

Figure 2-2 Lunar Data in an Ephemeris

To help you quickly identify lunar dates, Appendix A presents New Moon, Full Moon and Eclipse data for 2013 and 2014.

Full Moon, New Moon and the First Trade Date

The Moon has the greatest impact on those stocks that began trading for the very first time (the *first trade date*) on a financial exchange during a Full Moon or a New Moon. Appendix F lists first trade dates for the 60 largest stocks on the Toronto Stock Exchange and the 30 Dow Jones Industrial Index components. For a more complete listing of first trade dates, see the website www.investingsuccess.ca and look for the tab called Astrology. This tab contains a sub-section called First Trade Dates. Once a stock's first trade date is known, look up that date in an Ephemeris and see whether it coincides with either a Full or a New Moon. If the first trade date aligns with a New or Full Moon, then that stock is a good candidate for a lunar trading strategy.

Consider the example of Teck Resources which trades on the Toronto Stock Exchange under the ticker TSX:TCK/b. Teck Resources is a large global coal, iron ore and base metal miner with headquarters in Canada. Teck Resources made its debut onto the Toronto Stock Exchange on March 25, 1952, the date of a New Moon. The daily chart in Figure 2-3 illustrates the price action of Teck Resources for the 12 month period commencing September 2011. Dark shaded arrows denote New Moons while un-shaded arrows denote Full Moons.

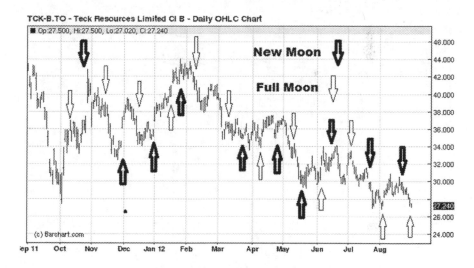

Figure 2-3 Teck Resources (TSX:TCK/b) daily chart

Note how New Moon and Full Moon dates align very closely with swings in price action. These lunar dates obviously do not account for 100% of all the price swings on the chart as there is only one New Moon and one Full Moon event each month. But the correlation between price inflection points and lunar events is uncanny nonetheless. Thus, when watching price action of Teck Resources, as a New Moon or Full Moon date draws near one should use technical chart analysis on short term charts to identify signs of a trend reversal that offers a short term trading opportunity.

Another example of this dynamic can be seen with Alliance Grain Traders which trades on the Toronto Stock Exchange under the ticker TSX:AGT. Alliance Grain Traders is a commodity trading firm based in western Canada specializing in brokering sales of cleaned and packaged peas, beans, lentils and chickpeas to the global marketplace. Alliance Grain Traders made its debut on the Toronto Stock Exchange September 18, 2009, a New Moon. The daily chart in Figure 2-4 illustrates the price action of Alliance Grain Traders for the 12 month period commencing September 2011. Dark shaded arrows denote New Moons while un-shaded arrows denote Full Moons.

Figure 2-4 Alliance Grain Traders (TSX:AGT) daily chart

Note how New Moon and Full Moon dates align very closely with swings in price action.

As these two examples illustrate, the Moon can have powerful effects on price action. The scientific explanation for this is deeper and more mysterious than I can explain. Thus, I simply use lunar occurrences as a compliment to my more mundane technical chart indicators.

In summary, to incorporate lunar phenomena into a trading strategy, one should identify companies that first traded on a New or a Full Moon date. Then, knowing that a Full Moon or New Moon date is approaching, use technical chart analysis with short term charts to watch for oversold or overbought conditions that may warrant a trade. Compiling a short list of trading candidates that had their first trade dates on a New or Full Moon will take some effort. To help you get started, Table 2-1 presents some Canadian and US listed companies.

Company	Ticker Symbol	First Trade Date	Lunar Influence
Central Fund	TSX: CEF.a	June 14, 1965	Full Moon
Corby	TSX: CDL.a	February 3, 1969	Full Moon
Cdn. Western Bank	TSX: CWB	May 14, 1984	Full Moon
Calian Technology	TSX: CTY	September 15, 1993	New Moon
Cinram	TSX: CRW.un	March 10, 1986	New Moon
Mullen Group	TSX: MTL	December 13, 1993	New Moon
Manulife	TSX: MFC	September 24, 1999	Full Moon
Pan Am Silver	TSX:PAA	October 9, 1984	Full Moon
Power Corp	TSX: PWF	October 10, 1984	Full Moon
Toromont	TSX: TIH	May 21, 1974	New Moon
West Fraser	TSX: WFT	May 7, 1986	New Moon
WestJet	TSX:WJA	July 12, 1999	New Moon
American Express	N: AXP	May 18, 1977	New Moon
Caterpillar	N:CAT	December 21, 1929	New Moon
Citigroup	N:C	December 4, 1998	Full Moon
Duke Energy	N:DUK	July 12, 1961	New Moon
Fed Ex	N:FDX	December 28, 1978	New Moon
General Electric	N: GE	May 27, 1956	Full Moon
Honeywell	N:HUN	September 19,1929	Full Moon
JP Morgan	N:JPM	April 1, 1969	Full Moon
Lockheed Martin	N:LMT	March 16, 1995	Full Moon
Merck	N: MRK	May 15, 1946	Full Moon
Nabors	N:NBR	November 3, 2005	New Moon
Tyson Foods	N:TSN	October 17, 1997	Full Moon

Table 2-1 Lunar first trade dates for several Canadian and US listed companies

Apogee and Perigee

Because of the Moon's slightly elliptical pattern of rotation around the Earth, there will be times when it is far from Earth and there will be times when it is close to Earth. The time when the Moon is farthest from Earth is called *apogee*. The time when the Moon is closest to Earth is called *perigee*.

New Zealand author Ken Ring in his book *Lunar Code* describes apogee and perigee in considerable detail. The following are some of his observations:

- Many, but not all, of the most severe global events occur within a few days of perigee.
- Fishing is good just before perigee, hopeless right on perigee and good again just after.
- Students seem to do better in exams when the Moon is in perigee, Full or New.
- If a First Quarter Moon coincides with a perigee, hurricanes are probable.
- When the summer Full Moon is in perigee or apogee, very warm temperatures may result.
- Perigee was always known and feared by ancient sailors because of the stormy weather and gales that invariably arrived. By far the greater number of cyclones, hurricanes, typhoons, volcanic eruptions, floods, heat waves and earthquakes in recorded history has been associated with a perigee or apogee.
- The apogee and perigee of the Moon have an effect on the tides on Earth. When the Moon is at apogee (the furthest distance from the Earth), it has less gravitational pull which contributes to lower tides or lower variation in the high/low tide level. When the Moon is at perigee (closer to the Earth), there is much more gravitational pull which contributes to the opposite effect: higher tides or greater variation in the high and low tide.

To further illustrate the effects of apogee and perigee, consider again the charts of Teck Resources and Alliance Grain Traders.

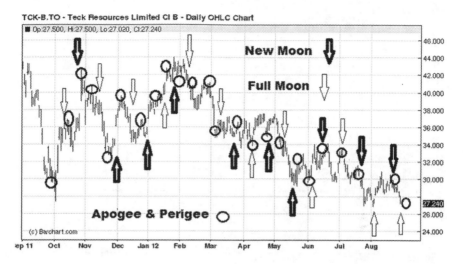

Figure 2-5 Teck Resources (TSX:TCK/b) apogee and perigee

The chart in Figure 2-5 is the same as the chart in Figure 2-3, but with apogee and perigee events overlaid as depicted by small circles. Notice how these apogee and perigee events tend to align themselves very closely with shorter swing changes in trend.

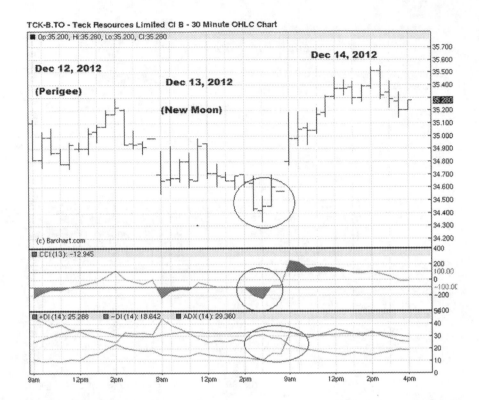

Figure 2-6 Teck Resources 30 minute chart

Shorter term charts function very well to focus on lunar events. Figure 2-6 illustrates a short term 30 minute chart for Teck Resources for the period December 12 through 14, 2012. On December 12, the Moon was at perigee and December 13 marked a New Moon. Note how at perigee price action reached a short term top and then proceeded to decline into a short term swing bottom the next day at the New Moon. A short term trader could have used technical indicators such as RSI, DMI and CCI in conjunction with these lunar events to time a trading entry into the stock.

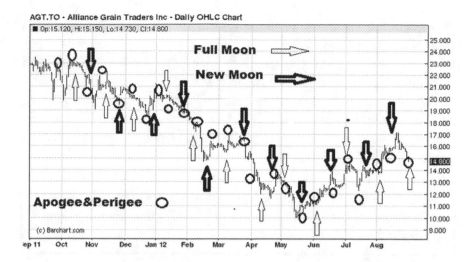

Figure 2-7 Alliance Grain Traders apogee and perigee

The chart in Figure 2-7 is the same as the chart in Figure 2-4, but with apogee and perigee events overlaid as depicted by small circles. Notice how these apogee and perigee events tend to align themselves very closely with shorter swing changes in trend.

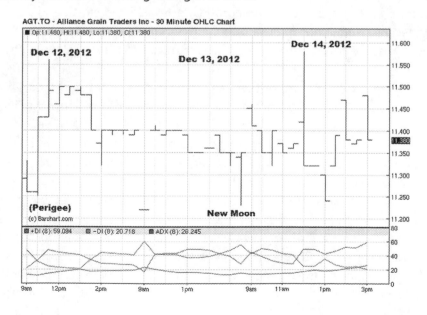

Figure 2-8 Alliance Grain Traders 30 minute chart

The chart in Figure 2-8 illustrates the 30 minute chart for Alliance Grain Traders for the period December 12, 2012 through December 14, 2012. Prior to this time span, the trend on Alliance Grain Traders had been decidedly down having fallen from above the $16 per share level over 3 months. A trader seeking to take a position in Alliance Grain Traders could have watched the price action start to bottom coming into December and then further used the above 30 minute chart as perigee and New Moon events drew close to time a suitable entry into the stock.

> For stocks having a first trade date falling at or very near a New Moon or Full Moon, use technical chart analysis and short term charts to watch for tradable events at New Moons, Full Moons, apogee or perigee events.

The North Node of Moon

As previously noted the Earth orbits the Sun in a plane called the ecliptic. The Moon orbits the Earth in its own plane. Mathematically, two planes that are not parallel must intersect. The intersection points between the Moon's lunar plane and Earth's ecliptic are termed the North and South nodes. Astrologers tend to focus on the North node and ephemeris tables clearly list the zodiacal position of the North Node for each calendar day.

Study the North Node positions and you will see that it moves in a backwards, retrograde pattern. The length of time for the North Node to make a full journey through the 12 signs of the zodiac is 18.6 years. As part of a trading or investing strategy, consider noting the times when the North Node changes signs of the zodiac, approximately every 1.55 years. The chart in Figure 2-9 illustrates monthly price behaviour of the S&P 500 Index dating back to 1998. On the chart, the circled areas depict the times when the North Node changed signs of the zodiac. Note how these times of sign change align closely with pivotal swing highs and lows including the market peak in 2000 and the peak that preceded the financial crisis of 2008. Definitely times for traders and investors to be alert. The North Node moved into the sign of Scorpio on August 29, 2012 and several weeks later the S&P 500 Index crested and began to decline as debates over the US 'fiscal cliff' intensified. The North Node will remain in the sign of Scorpio until February 2014.

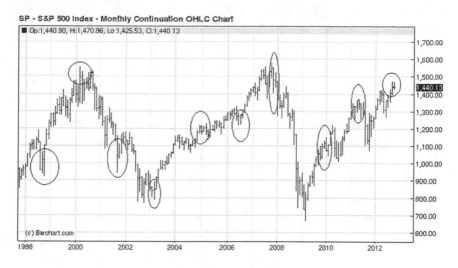

Figure 2-9 S&P 500 Index—North Node changing signs

Watch major market indices for trend changes as the North Node of Moon changes signs of the Zodiac every 1.55 years.

Solar and Lunar Eclipses

A solar eclipse occurs when the Moon passes between the Sun and Earth and fully or partially blocks the Sun. This can happen only at a New Moon, when the Sun and the Moon are in conjunction and only when the New Moon occurs close to one of the Nodes. Because the Moon's lunar orbit plane intersects with the ecliptic plane at the two Nodes that are 180 degrees apart, New Moons occur close to the nodes at two periods of the year approximately six months (173.3 days) apart, known as *eclipse seasons*. There will always be at least one solar eclipse during an eclipse season. Sometimes the New Moon occurs close enough to a node during each of two consecutive months to eclipse the Sun in two partial eclipses. This means that in any given year, there will always be at least two solar eclipses, but there could be as many as five.

A lunar eclipse occurs when the Sun, Earth, and Moon are aligned exactly, or very closely so, with the Earth in the middle. The Earth blocks the Sun's rays from striking the Moon. This can only happen at a Full Moon. Eclipse dates should be watched closely as price trend changes often occur at these dates. The chart in Figure 2-10 illustrates monthly price behaviour of the S&P 500 futures dating back 15 years. The circles on the chart depict many of the solar and lunar eclipse dates. Notice how these dates align quite well with swings in price action. Appendix A provides eclipse data for 2013 through 2014. Using technical chart analysis, watch as eclipse dates approach. If you see oversold or overbought conditions that could lend themselves to a trend reversal, be prepared to take action accordingly.

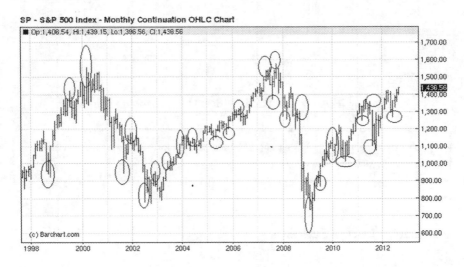

Figure 2-10 S&P 500 Index—Solar and Lunar eclipses

The chart illustrated in Figure 2-11 is an hourly snapshot of the Dow Jones Industrial Average around the time frame of June 4, 2012, the date of a partial lunar eclipse and the date of a market swing low. A trader seeking to enter a trade on Dow futures could have watched the developing technical negative divergence and the rising ADX feature to time an entry position.

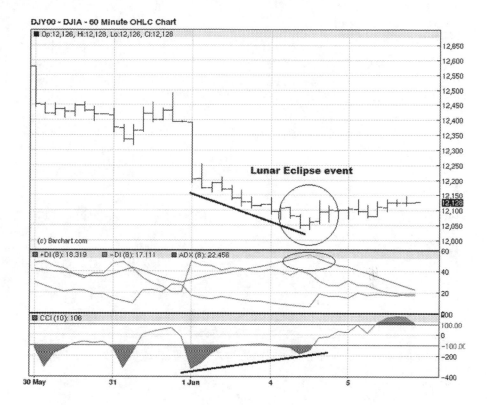

Figure 2-11 Dow Jones Industrial Average hourly
chart June 4, 2012

On a similar note, the chart in Figure 2-12 illustrates the Dow Jones Industrial Average around the period of November 13, 2012 the date of a solar eclipse and a swing high point on price action.

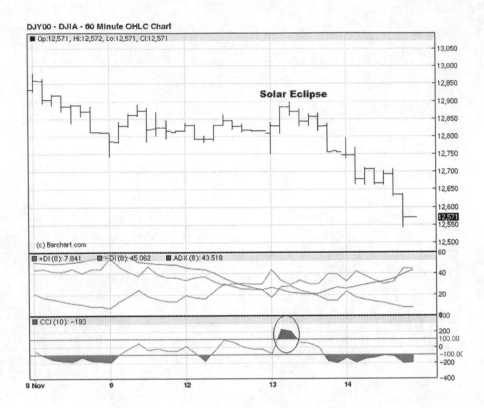

Figure 2-12 Dow Jones Industrial Average hourly chart
November 13, 2012

Watch major market indices to exhibit trend changes during solar and lunar eclipse events.

Next, let us turn our attention to an examination of how planetary astrology can be incorporated into a trading strategy.

CHAPTER THREE

Planetary Trading

There are eight planets that form the framework for the application of astrology to trading and investing on the financial markets. These planets are Mercury, Venus, Mars, Jupiter, Saturn, Uranus, Neptune and Pluto. In recent years there has been much debate as to whether or not Pluto qualifies as a true planet or simply one of several dwarf planets. For the purposes of this book, consider Pluto to be a true planet.

This chapter looks at how planetary aspects, first trade dates and synodic periods all can be incorporated into a trading strategy.

Planets and Aspects

The diagram in Figure 3-1 courtesy of www.zoomschool.com shows the positional arrangement of the planets in relation to the Sun. Note also the sizes of the other planets in comparison to Earth.

Figure 3-1 The Planets

From a vantage point located on Earth, as these planets orbit 360 degrees around the Sun, they can be seen to make angles (called aspects) to the Sun and to each other. The aspects commonly used to study the financial markets are 0, 30, 45, 60, 90, 120 and 180 degrees (respectively called *conjunct, semi-sextile, semi-square, sextile, square, trine and opposition* events). The application of astrology to market trading allows for some 'room' (or orb) when considering the various aspects.

- A conjunct event (0 degree separation) is deemed to be occurring when two planets are within 10 degrees of being 0 degrees apart from each other.
- The same applies to an opposition event (180 degree separation).
- A square event (90 degree separation) is deemed to be occurring when two planets are within 5 degrees of being 90 degrees to one another.
- A semi-sextile event (30 degree separation) event is deemed to be occurring when two planets are within 3 degrees of being 30 degrees from one another.
- A semi-square event (45 degree separation) is deemed to be occurring when two planets are with 3 degrees of being 45 degrees apart from one another.
- A sextile event (60 degree separation) is deemed to be occurring when two planets are with 5 degrees of being 60 degrees apart from one another.
- A trine event (120 degree separation) is deemed to be occurring when two planets are with 5 degrees of being 120 degrees apart from one another.

Strange Symbols and the Ephemeris

Figure 3-2 presents a summary of the symbols used in astrology to denote the various planets and the various aspects. As you repeatedly apply the information in this book to your market activity, you will become quite fluent with these strange looking symbols, called *glyphs*.

Figure 3-3 presents an excerpt taken from a heliocentric Ephemeris for the month of December 1980. Notice how the symbols denoting the various planets appear along the top of the data table. Along the left axis, the days of the month appear. In each column notice the number expressed in degrees along with a glyph. Thus, for any given day in the month of December 1980, one can find the position of the Moon and the various planets in terms of degrees and astrological sign. For example, on December 1, 1980 we can see that: Jupiter was 26 degrees, 45 minutes into the sign of Virgo. On December 20, Venus was 25 degrees and 17 minutes into the sign of Libra. With a little practice, you will quite soon find yourself comfortably interpreting the data in an ephemeris. In my experience, a good heliocentric ephemeris is not something readily available in book stores. I do have one for calendar years 2000 and onwards. However, I find it just as easy to obtain my heliocentric data from the website **www.astro.com/swisseph/swepha_e.htm.**

Points		Zodiac Signs		Aspects	
☉	Sun	♈ Aries		♂	0° Conjunction
☽	Moon	♉ Taurus			Occultation, Tight ♂
☿	Mercury	♊ Gemini			Cazimi, ☉ eclipse
♀	Venus	♋ Cancer		⚺	30° Semi-sextile
⊕	Earth	♌ Leo		∠	45° Semi-square
♂	Mars	♍ Virgo		✳	60° Sextile
⚳	Ceres	♎ Libra		□	90° Square
♃	Jupiter	♏ Scorpio		△	120° Trine
♄	Saturn	♐ Sagittarius			135° Sesquisquare
⚷	Chiron	♑ Capricorn		⚻	150° Quincunx
♅	Uranus	♒ Aquarius		☍	180° Opposition
♆	Neptune	♓ Pisces			
♇ Pluto					
☊	North Node				

Figure 3-2 Astrology Symbols

DECEMBER 1980   **00:00 UT heliocentric**

Day	Sid.t	Terra	☽	☿	♀	♂	♃	♄	♅	♆	♇	☿
M 1	4 40 1	8♊57'07	9♊ 6	9♎33	24♍36	25♋53	26♍45	2♎32	26♏ 1	22♐19	22♎ 2	16♉ 6
T 2	4 43 57	9°57'58	10° 6	13°12	26°13	26°29	26°49	2°34	26° 2	22°19	22° 2	16° 6
W 3	4 47 54	10°58'50	11° 6	16°46	27°50	27° 6	26°54	2°36	26° 3	22°20	22° 3	16° 7
T 4	4 51 50	11°59'43	12° 6	20°15	29°28	27°43	26°58	2°38	26° 4	22°20	22° 3	16° 8
F 5	4 55 47	13° 0'37	13° 5	23°38	1♎ 5	28°19	27° 3	2°40	26° 4	22°20	22° 3	16° 9
S 6	4 59 43	14° 1'33	14° 4	26°57	2°42	28°56	27° 7	2°42	26° 5	22°21	22° 4	16° 9
S 7	5 3 40	15° 2'29	15° 4	0♏11	4°19	29°33	27°12	2°44	26° 6	22°21	22° 4	16°10
M 8	5 7 36	16° 3'27	16° 3	3°22	5°56	0♒10	27°17	2°46	26° 7	22°21	22° 5	16°11
T 9	5 11 33	17° 4'26	17° 2	6°29	7°33	0°47	27°21	2°48	26° 7	22°22	22° 5	16°11
W10	5 15 30	18° 5'25	18° 1	9°33	9°10	1°24	27°26	2°50	26° 8	22°22	22° 6	16°12
T11	5 19 26	19° 6'25	19° 1	12°34	10°47	2° 1	27°30	2°52	26° 9	22°23	22° 6	16°13
F12	5 23 23	20° 7'26	20° 0	15°32	12°24	2°38	27°35	2°54	26°10	22°23	22° 6	16°14
S13	5 27 19	21° 8'28	21° 1	18°28	14° 1	3°15	27°39	2°56	26°10	22°23	22° 7	16°14
S 14	5 31 16	22° 9'30	22° 1	21°22	15°37	3°52	27°44	2°58	26°11	22°24	22° 7	16°15
M15	5 35 12	23°10'32	23° 2	24°13	17°14	4°29	27°48	3° 0	26°12	22°24	22° 8	16°16
T16	5 39 9	24°11'35	24° 3	27° 3	18°51	5° 6	27°53	3° 2	26°13	22°24	22° 8	16°16
W17	5 43 5	25°12'38	25° 5	29°52	20°28	5°44	27°58	3° 4	26°13	22°25	22° 9	16°17
T 18	5 47 2	26°13'41	26° 7	2♐40	22° 4	6°21	28° 2	3° 6	26°14	22°25	22° 9	16°18
F 19	5 50 59	27°14'45	27°10	5°26	23°41	6°58	28° 7	3° 8	26°15	22°25	22° 9	16°19
S 20	5 54 55	28°15'49	28°12	8°12	25°17	7°36	28°11	3°10	26°15	22°26	22°10	16°19
S 21	5 58 52	29°16'54	29°15	10°57	26°54	8°13	28°16	3°12	26°16	22°26	22°10	16°20
M22	6 2 48	0♋17'59	0♋18	13°42	28°30	8°50	28°20	3°14	26°17	22°26	22°11	16°21
T23	6 6 45	1°19'05	1°22	16°26	0♏ 7	9°28	28°25	3°16	26°18	22°27	22°11	16°22
W24	6 10 41	2°20'11	2°24	19°11	1°43	10° 5	28°29	3°18	26°18	22°27	22°11	16°22
T 25	6 14 38	3°21'17	3°27	21°56	3°20	10°43	28°34	3°20	26°19	22°28	22°12	16°23
F 26	6 18 34	4°22'24	4°30	24°41	4°56	11°20	28°39	3°22	26°20	22°28	22°12	16°24
S 27	6 22 31	5°23'32	5°32	27°28	6°32	11°58	28°43	3°24	26°21	22°28	22°13	16°24
S 28	6 26 28	6°24'40	6°34	0♑15	8° 8	12°35	28°48	3°27	26°21	22°29	22°13	16°25
M29	6 30 24	7°25'48	7°35	3° 3	9°44	13°13	28°52	3°29	26°22	22°29	22°14	16°26
T 30	6 34 21	8°26'57	8°36	5°52	11°21	13°51	28°57	3°31	26°23	22°29	22°14	16°27
W31	6 38 17	9♋28'07	9♋37	8♑43	12♏57	14♒28	29♍ 1	3♎33	26♏24	22♐30	22♎14	16♉27

Delta T = 51.31 sec.   created from Swiss Ephemeris, Copyright Astrodienst AG [26.5.2006]

Figure 3-3 Ephemeris page December 1980

Case Study #1—Apple (Nasdaq:AAPL)

The best way to see astrology in action is to look at a case study for a particular stock. In Figure 3-3, look at the date of December 12, 1980. On that date, the data shows that Mercury was at 15 degrees of Scorpio, Venus was at 12 degrees of Libra, Mars at 2 degrees of Aquarius, Jupiter at 27 degrees of Virgo, Saturn at 2 degrees of Libra, Uranus at 26 degrees of Scorpio, Neptune at 22 degrees of Sagittarius and Pluto was at 22 degrees of Libra.

The date of December 12, 1980 happens to be the day when shares in Apple (Nasdaq:AAPL) first started trading on a recognized stock exchange. This date is Apple's first trade date.

When applying astrology to an individual stock, the first step is to compose a visual diagram of the positions of the Planets on the first trade date. To construct such a diagram, one could start with a blank version of a diagram similar to that of Figure 1-1 shown back in Chapter 1. But, thankfully technological advances have touched upon the world of astrology. Software programs are now available to prepare first trade charts for you. I personally have two programs that I use. The first is produced by AIR Software and is called *Millenium Trax*, the second is produced by Astrolabe and is called *Solar Fire Gold*. Both are very affordable. I am sure there are many more such programs available for purchase and indeed one may even find apps for smart phones and tablets that will help you with astrology charts.

When running one of these programs, the entry data required consists of the first trade date, the location and a time. If the stock happens to be a US traded equity, the location will be New York. Canadian equities will have a location of Toronto and U.K. equities would have a location of London and so on. The time element will be the time the stock started trading on the first trade date. I always assume the time element to be the hour at which the stock exchange starts its trading. Sometimes there can be delays in getting a new stock up and trading for the first time, but this tends to be the exception. For US and Canada, trade start times are taken to be 9:30 am. With date, time and location data entered into the program, the result will be a chart showing the placements of the planets on that date. Although termed a first trade chart, such a chart is technically called a *horoscope* derived from the Greek *horoskopis* meaning 'a look at the hours'. The following figure shows the chart generated for Apple (Nasdaq:AAPL) using the *Millenium Trax* software. Note that when entering data parameters for a first trade chart, you must specify whether you are wanting the heliocentric calculations or the geocentric calculations. In the case of Apple (Nasdaq:AAPL), I have selected heliocentric.

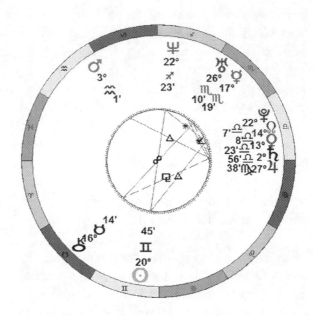

APPLE (Nasdaq:AAPL)
Dec 12 1980 9:3000
TZ=5 W
⊙ 05 10,1980
⊙ 02 04,1981

Figure 3-4 Apple (Nasdaq:AAPL) heliocentric first trade chart

After generating a first trade chart, the second step is to study it carefully and note the planetary pairs that form aspects.

In the Apple (Nasdaq:AAPL) heliocentric chart one can see that:

- Sun is 180 degrees from Neptune which is an opposition event.
- Sun and Pluto are 122 degrees apart which is a trine event.
- Mars and Saturn are 121 degrees apart for a trine event.
- Mercury and Saturn are 45 degrees apart for a semi-square event.
- Neptune and Pluto are 60 degrees apart for a sextile event.
- Jupiter and Sun are 97 degrees apart which is just a bit too much for a square event.
- Mercury and Pluto are 25 degrees apart which is not quite a semi-sextile event.
- Jupiter and Mars are 126 degrees part which is too much for a trine event.
- Sun and Venus are 113 degrees apart which is not enough for a trine event.

The third step is to determine which of the aspects is the most powerful to incorporate into a trading or investing strategy. To make this determination, focus on the aspects made between the faster moving inner planets (Mercury, Venus, Mars) with the Sun and aspects between these faster moving planets and the outer, slower moving planets. Focus also on any aspects between the slower outer planets and the Sun.

Fourth, use either an ephemeris table or a software program to generate a list of such aspects dating back several years.

Fifth, generate a stock chart of the stock in question going back several years. Mark the aspect dates on the price chart and see which aspects most often align with a swing high or swing low trend changes in price. Once it has been determined which aspects align most often with price swings, these aspects can then be used to look forward in time and anticipate when they will repeat themselves and deliver a swing change in price trend.

Continuing with the study of Apple (Nasdaq:AAPL), the aspects involving Sun-Neptune, Sun-Pluto, Mars-Saturn, Mercury-Saturn and Neptune-Pluto all appear to be excellent candidates to focus on. However, given that Neptune and Pluto are both slower moving outer planets, we can discard them from the list. Figure 3-5 presents a daily chart of Apple (Nasdaq:AAPL) from October 2011 to October 2012. Notice how a Mercury-Saturn 45 degree aspect occurs in very close proximity to swing highs made in October, April and at the $705 peak in September. Traders engaged in AAPL stock and watching chart technical analysis would have had an extra measure of fore-warning at these swing highs. The daily chart in Figure 3-6 covers the same time frame and shows additional aspects that traders would have been alert to. And so it goes. This is how astrological aspects as determined from a first trade chart can be used as a very powerful compliment to the technical analysis techniques already being as part of your trading.

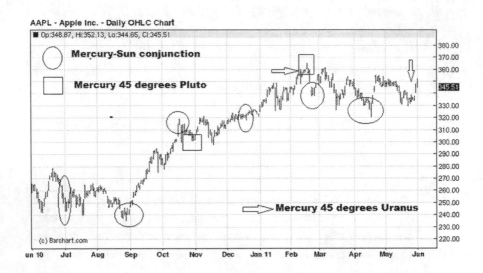

Figure 3-5 Aspects affecting (Nasdaq:AAPL) share price

Figure 3-6 More aspects affecting (Nasdaq:AAPL) share price

Case Study #2—Ford Motor Company (NYSE:F)

As another case study, consider the Ford Motor Company. Figure 3-7 illustrates the first trade chart for Ford generated using the Millenium Trax software. In this case study, I am using geocentric astrology to show you how it differs slightly from its heliocentric counterpart.

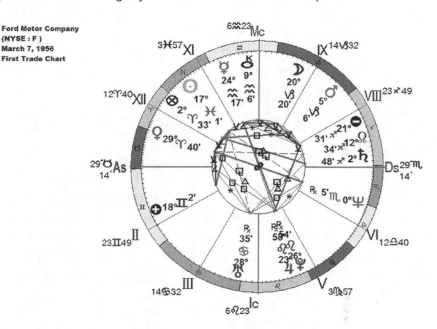

Figure 3-7 Ford Motor Company (NYSE:F)
geocentric first trade chart

There are four aspects that immediately stand out on this chart. Venus is 180 degrees opposite to Neptune, Mercury is opposite Pluto, Mercury is opposite Saturn and Venus is 90 degrees square to Uranus.

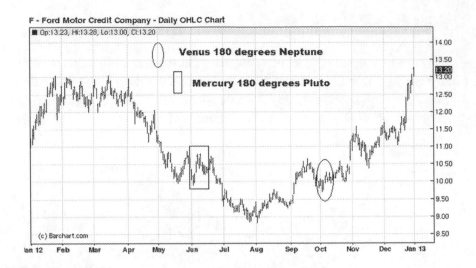

Figure 3-8 Aspects affecting (NYSE:F)

Figure 3-8 illustrates a daily price chart of Ford Motor Company dating back 12 months. Note in mid-June 2012, share price action experienced a reversal at the Mercury-Pluto opposition, after failing to get above the late-May highs. In early October, price action registered a swing bottom thus giving traders who missed the late August bottom another chance to take long positions.

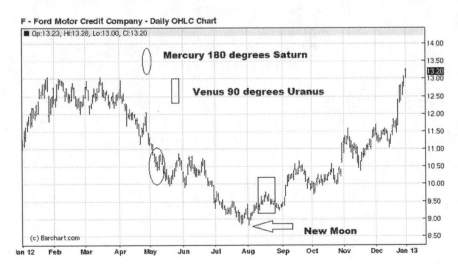

Figure 3-9 More aspects affecting (NYSE:F)

Figure 3-9 illustrates the Mercury-Saturn and Venus-Uranus aspects. The Mercury-Saturn aspect in May aligns with what appears to be a short-covering rally. The swing high in August would have been a good point for short term traders to take profits assuming long positions had been initiated in early August as a New Moon appeared.

The aspects illustrated in the preceding two figures do not capture all the swings in price. But when used in conjunction with technical chart analysis, these aspects will provide you with a unique perspective on the price action of Ford Motor Company shares.

Five Steps for Applying Astrology to Individual Stocks

1. Compile a first trade date astrology chart for the stock in question.
2. Note the planetary pairs that form aspects.
3. Determine which of these aspects have the most powerful impact on price.
4. Generate a list of these aspects going back several years.
5. Overlay these aspects on a stock chart going back several years to verify their effectiveness. Then, watch for these aspects to re-occur in the future.

Ruler-Ship, Exaltation, Fall and Detriment

Astrology also rests firmly on the notions of *ruler-ship*, *exaltation*, *detriment* and *fall*. Each sign of the zodiac is deemed to be 'ruled' by a planet or planetary pair. That is, the particular zodiac sign will exhibit characteristics similar to its ruling planet or planetary pair. For a given zodiac sign (or point within a sign), certain planets function very well and exhibit powerful influence. This powerful influence is called *exaltation*. There are also signs in which a given planet may exhibit unpredictable behavior thus keeping traders and investors on edge. This is behaviour is called *detriment*. Lastly, there are signs where planets exhibit very weak amounts of influence. This weak influence is called *fall*.

Table 3-1 shows the *ruler-ship* of the various signs along with positions of *exaltation*, *fall* and *detriment*. Notice that when a planet is in *exaltation* in a sign, it will be in *fall* when it reaches the opposing sign of the zodiac. A planet will be in *fall* when it appears in a sign opposite to that sign which it rules. For example, if Jupiter figures prominently in the price moves of a stock, it would be wise to pay close attention to price action of that stock as Jupiter experiences *exaltation* in the sign of Cancer. Table 3-1 suggests that the point of 5 degrees Cancer should be focused on. Some older literature studied when researching this book was adamant that *exaltation* and *fall* only occurred at certain degrees of a sign, while other publications took a slightly more relaxed stance and considered *exaltation* and *fall* to occur during the entire transit of the sign. If Venus figures prominently in the price moves of a stock, take note that Venus is in *detriment* as it passes through the signs of Aries and Scorpio, so any favourable price action you may be expecting may be somewhat dampened. Thus, when incorporating the notions of *exaltation*, *detriment* and *fall* into your trading strategy, be sure to do adequate back-testing to see how price action has responded in past across the entire transit of a sign as well as at the specific points listed in Table 3-1. Back testing can be done with the help of ephemeris tables or with a software program.

Sign	Ruler	Exaltation	Fall	Detriment
Aries	Mars/Pluto	Sun 19 degrees	Saturn 21 degrees	Venus
Taurus	Venus	Moon 3 degrees	Uranus	Mars
Gemini	Mercury	Mercury		Jupiter
Cancer	Moon	Jupiter 5 degrees	Mars 28 degrees	Saturn
Leo	Sun	Neptune	Pluto	Uranus
Virgo	Mercury	Mercury 15 degrees	Venus 27 degrees	Neptune
Libra	Venus	Saturn 21 degrees	Sun 19 degrees	Mars/Pluto
Scorpio	Mars	Uranus	Moon 3 degrees	Venus
Sagittarius	Jupiter	South Node 3 degrees	Mercury	Mercury
Capricorn	Saturn	Mars 28 degrees	Jupiter 5 degrees	Moon
Aquarius	Uranus/Saturn	Pluto	Neptune	Sun
Pisces	Neptune/Jupiter	Venus 27 degrees	Mercury 15 degrees	Mercury

Table 3-1 Exaltation, Detriment and Fall Positions

Looking once again at our example of Apple (Nasdaq:AAPL), we can clearly see the influences of *exaltation*. Using the ephemeris tables, I determined the calendar dates for several of the above *exaltation* dates that fell into the timeframe August 2011 to August 2012. Figure 3-10 plots these dates.

Figure 3-10 Exaltation dates

Notice how the Sun at 19 degrees of Aries position aligns with a major swing high in April 2012. See the rally that got underway early in October 2011. This rally stumbled for a while as Saturn entered its exalted time at 21 degrees of Libra. Saturn has a reputation for spoiling the party and in this case it lived up to its reputation. Lastly, Venus entered its point of *exaltation* in February 2012. Price was already rallying at that time, but look closely and you will see that as Venus hit its point of *exaltation*, price action surged quickly. Although not shown on this chart, Mercury hit 15 degrees Virgo and *exaltation* on September 9, 2012. Price action of AAPL the very next day fell some $18 per share in true 'mercurial' fashion!

On September 21, 2012 when AAPL hit its high of $705, it is curious to observe that Saturn was at 28 degrees of Libra, just past its maximum point of *exaltation*. Saturn typically can have a detrimental effect on share price action and in this case, it seems that once the all-time was reached, Saturn exerted its powerful suppressing nature to drive price action downwards. As well, at the time of this price high, Mars was in the sign of Scorpio where it rules. Mars having war-like tendency, seems to have declared war on share price as AAPL went on to lose nearly $200 per share in value by the end of 2012. Lastly, at the time of the $705 high, Jupiter was at 16 degrees Gemini. Jupiter typically is associated with expansive behaviours and by being in Gemini, it was in *fall*, thus its expansionary tendencies were muted, giving added impetus to a fall in share price.

Although using planetary phenomena in market trading requires considerable preparation work, once you have done the preparation work for your favorite stocks or commodity futures, you stand to enjoy a distinct advantage in your trading. This advantage can then be further sharpened by using synodic periods, sign changes, retrograde motion and Mid-Heaven and Ascendant techniques which we now will examine in greater detail.

> Watch for significant price movements at those times when planets are in *exaltation, detriment* or *fall*.

Mid-Heaven and Ascendant Strategies

In Chapter One, the concepts of Mid-Heaven (MC) and Ascendant (Asc) were introduced. To use the notion of Mid-Heaven in a trading strategy, it is also necessary to generate a geocentric first trade chart. The chart in Figure 3-11 is that of Coca Cola (NYSE:KO) which has a first trade date of September 26, 1924.

On this or any geocentric first trade chart, the Mid-Heaven is at the top of the chart. In the case of Coca Cola, the Mid-Heaven (MC) is at 29 degrees of the Sign of Leo.

Each calendar year, traders should make careful note of when the faster moving planets Mercury and Venus pass across the Mid-Heaven position found in a stock's first trade chart. Slightly slower moving Mars can also be important too. Within one or two degrees on either side of the MC position watch stock price action for possible swing reversals in trend. Sometime such swings can be short in duration, sometimes larger.

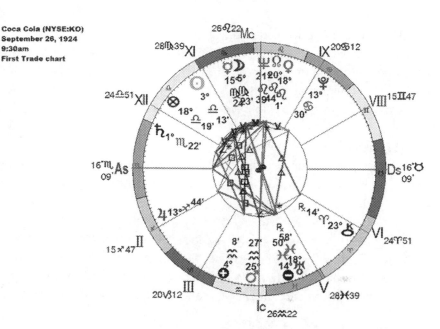

Figure 3-11 Coca Cola (NYSE:KO) first trade chart

The Ascendant (denoted Asc) on a geocentric first trade chart such as the one in Figure 3-11 is taken as being at the 9 o'clock position. Each calendar year, traders should make careful note of when the faster moving planets Mercury and Venus pass across the Ascendant. Watch too what slightly slower Mars does. Within one day on either side of these dates observe share price action closely for possible swing reversals in trend. Sometime such swings can be short in duration, sometimes larger.

In the case of Coca Cola, the planet Mercury in 2011 passed over the Mid-Heaven position of 29 degrees Leo on July 27, turned retrograde, passed over the point 29 Leo on August 9, turned direct and again passed over 29 Leo on September 9, 2011. The chart in Figure 3-12 depicts daily price action covering these dates. Note how these MC crossing dates align with price tops and price swings.

Venus in 2011 passed over the Mid-Heaven on August 21 and Mars crossed the Mid-Heaven on November 10. The chart in Figure 3-13 depicts hourly price action covering the time frame around August 21, 2011. Note how Venus crossing the MC of Coca Cola aligns with a very nice tradable dip in price action that a trader or investor could have been tracking. The chart in Figure 3-14 depicts hourly price action covering the time frame around November 10, 2011. Note how Mars crossing the MC of Coca Cola aligns with another very nice tradable dip in price action that a trader or investor could have been watching for.

In 2012, Mercury passed over the Mid-Heaven on September 1 and Venus on October 3. Although not shown here, the charts for these time frames also show interesting swings in price action. Slower moving Mars will not pass the Mid-Heaven in 2012.

In 2011, Mercury passed over the Ascendant (Asc) on October 24, Venus on October 22. Slower moving Mars did not pass the Ascendant (Asc). Figure 3-15 depicts hourly price action covering this period. Notice the rise and fall of price action as Mercury and Venus crossed the Ascendant.

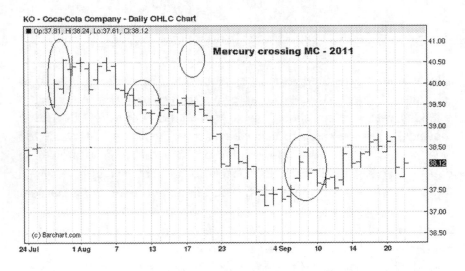

Figure 3-12 Coca Cola (NYSE:KO) Mercury across MC

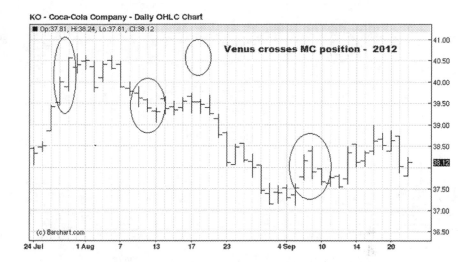

Figure 3-13 Coca Cola (NYSE:KO) Venus across the MC

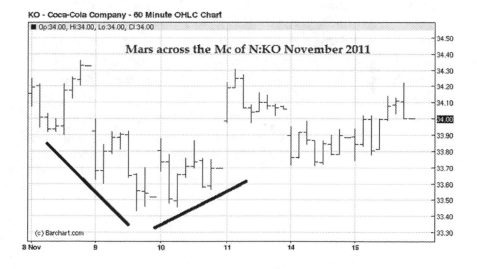

Figure 3-14 Coca Cola (NYSE:KO) Mars across the MC

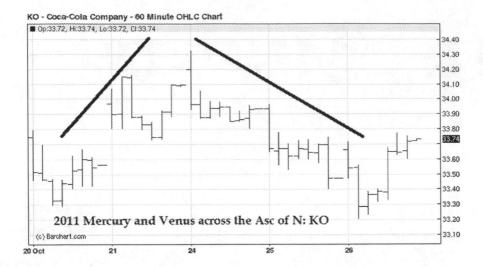

KO - Coca-Cola Company - 60 Minute OHLC Chart

2011 Mercury and Venus across the Asc of N: KO

(c) Barchart.com

Figure 3-15 Coca Cola (NYSE:KO) Mercury and
Venus across the Asc

In 2012, Mercury passed the Mid-Heaven on October 17, Venus on December 5 and Mars on September 17. The chart in Figure 3-16 illustrates price action covering the period mid-September 2012 to mid-October, 2012. The bottom pane on the chart is the Commodity Channel Index (CCI), a standard technical indicator used to denote overbought and oversold conditions. Mars crossed the Ascendant on September 17 and one day later, intra-day price action hit an overbought peak. Mercury crossed the Ascendant on October 17, a critical line of support was breached and CCI crossed below the 'minus 100' mark. An alert trader watching this unfold could have taken advantage accordingly.

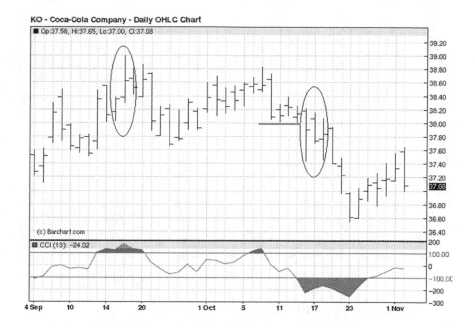

Figure 3-16 Coca Cola (NYSE:KO) Mars and
Mercury across the Asc

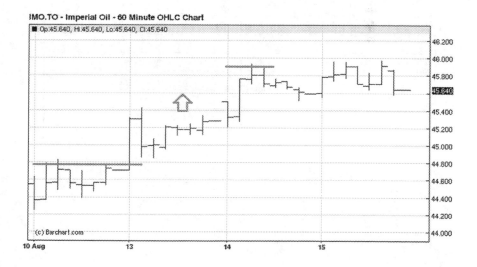

Figure 3-17 Imperial Oil (TSX:IMO) 60 minute chart

As another example, consider Imperial Oil, a large Canadian integrated oil concern which trades on the Toronto Stock Exchange under the ticker symbol TSX:IMO. The chart in Figure 3-14 shows hourly price action for Imperial Oil during the timeframe of August 13, 2012. Although the first trade chart is not displayed, the Mid-Heaven for Imperial Oil is at 23 degrees of Libra. Mars crossed over this Mid-Heaven position on August 13, 2012. An alert trader using technical chart analysis and short term charts would have noted a breakout above a line of resistance and then a run up in price of $1 a share.

> Watch for significant price moves when the planets, Mercury, Venus and Mars cross the Asc and MC first trade chart positions of stocks.

Trading using Synodic Cycles

Each of the planets orbits the Sun with a different period of revolution as Table 3-2 shows. Mercury being close to the Sun completes its orbit very quickly. Pluto being far away from the Sun takes a good long while to complete an orbit.

Planet	Synodic Orbital Period Around Sun
Mercury	88 days
Venus	225 days
Earth	365 days
Mars	687 days
Jupiter	11.85 years
Saturn	29.42 years
Uranus	83.75 years
Neptune	163.74 years
Pluto	245.33 years

Table 3-2 Planet-Sun synodic periods

A synodic cycle is that length of time for a celestial body to complete an entire pattern as referenced from the fixed observation point of the

Sun (heliocentric). Such a pattern is usually taken to mean the time from when a planet is conjunct (0 degrees) to Earth to when it is again conjunct Earth. Such a pattern could also be the time from when a planet is conjunct (0 degrees) another planet to when it is again conjunct that planet. Table 3-3 presents various planet to planet synodic cycles. A synodic cycle between two planets is given by S = (s1 x s2)/(s2-s1), where s1 and s2 are the times to orbit the Sun as taken from Table 3-2 previous.

	Earth	Mercury	Venus	Mars	Jupiter	Saturn	Uranus	Neptune	Pluto
Mercury	116 days		144.5 days	100.9 days	89.8 days	88.7 days	88.2 days	88.1 days	88.0 days
Venus	584 days	144.5 days		334.5 days	237.3 days	229.8 days	226.6 days	225.8 days	225.5 days
Mars	780 days	100.9 days	334.5 days		2.23 years	2.0 years	1.92 years	1.90 years	1.90 years
Jupiter	399 days	89.8 days	237.3 days	2.23 years		19.85 years	13.81 years	12.77 years	12.45 years
Saturn	376 days	88.7 days	229.8 days	2.0 years	19.85 years		45.26 years	35.68 years	33.40 years
Uranus	370 days	88.2 days	226.6 days	1.92 years	13.81 years	45.26 years		171.42 years	127.15 years
Neptune	367 days	88.1 days	225.8 days	1.90 years	12.77 years	35.68 years	171.42 years		492.34 years
Pluto	367 days	88.0 days	225.5 days	1.90 years	12.45 years	33.40 years	127.15 years	492.34 years	

Table 3-3 Planet-Planet synodic periods

As Table 3-3 shows, Saturn and Jupiter have a 19.85 year synodic orbital period. The 0, 90 and 180 degree aspects are important to follow for market traders. Consider the following historical heliocentric developments. Saturn was 0 degrees separated from Jupiter for the first 8 months of 1961. During 1961, the Dow Jones Industrials peaked at near 734 before declining to the 580 level for a drop of about 20 percent. In 1970 and into early 1971, Saturn and Jupiter came into a 180 degree aspect on a number of occasions. During this time frame the Dow Jones Industrials registered a significant low after making a 285 point drop (28 percent) from a high in 1968. From late-1975 to mid-1976 Saturn and Jupiter came into a 90 degree aspect on several occasions and the Dow Jones Industrials rallied hard and fast from a significant low made late in

1974. In the first half of 1981, Saturn and Jupiter again enjoyed a 0 degree aspect, the first such occurrence since 1961. This time frame marked a peak in the Dow Jones Industrial Average. Interestingly enough, following this peak, a sell-off of some 24% took place which cleared the decks for the start of a major bull market run. From May to September 2000, Saturn and Jupiter again arrived at a 0 degree aspect some 19 years after the last such aspect. This aspect came just as the Dow Jones Industrials was reaching a major high. In the first part of 2006 Saturn and Jupiter were at a 90 degree aspect and markets had an 8 percent decline before resuming an uptrend. From late 2010 through May 2011, Saturn and Jupiter were at a 180 degree aspect. During this period the market rallied smartly only to peak and fade in May just as this aspect was concluding. Saturn and Jupiter are scheduled to make a 90 degree aspect again from mid-2015 to the end of 2015. Traders and investors should be mindful of this timeframe for a possible significant turn in trend.

In addition to the 0, 90 and 180 degree aspects, breaking the Saturn Jupiter synodic cycle of 19.85 years into smaller increments can also give a unique perspective on market behaviour. Table 3-4 presents some of these smaller subdivisions.

Sub-Division of Saturn-Jupiter cycle	Expressed in terms of months of time
19.85 / 4	59.6 months
19.85 / 5	47.7 months
19.85 / 6	39.7 months
19.85 / 7	34 months
19.85/ 8	29.8 months
19.85 / 9	26.5 months

Table 3-4 Saturn-Jupiter cycle sub-divided

Consider that in 2002 the S&P futures bottomed on October 7. Projecting ahead 59.6 months takes one to the start of October 2007. The markets registered a notable secondary high on October 8, 2007. From this same 2002 low, projecting ahead 34 months takes one to early August 2005 and in fact markets registered a swing high at this very time which was not challenged until 3 months later. Projecting ahead 29.8 months reveals a swing bottom in April 2005. And lastly projecting forward 26.5 months places one in December 2004 when markets peaked. This peak was not bested until 8 months later.

From the October 2007 high, projecting forward 29.8 months takes one to a swing high early in 2010. Projecting ahead 34 months takes one to the low for 2010. Projecting ahead 47.7 months takes one to the October 2011 lows. Projecting ahead 59.6 months takes one to September 2012 during which North American indices hit a peak.

Studying some of the longer synodic periods between various planets is an interesting exercise and one that I enjoy engaging in frequently using both individual stocks and market indices. While these longer synodic periods may not be of help with short term trading, they may help explain some of the longer term price cycles we have seen unfold over the years. For further information to ponder, consider that financial markets registered a significant peak in 1929 and a significant low in 1974. Is this a 45 year Saturn-Uranus synodic period in action? In 2000 the markets registered a significant high and a significant low in early 2009. Is this one-half of a Jupiter-Saturn synodic period? Markets registered a low in late 2002 and a significant low in early 2009. Is this one-half of a Jupiter-Uranus synodic period? My research into these longer cycles is ongoing and will likely form the subject matter of a separate book to be published in the near future.

> Synodic periods are a fascinating phenomenon. Studying longer term market price action in terms of synodic periods can assist the trader in seeing the markets from a different perspective.

Trading using Retrograde Periods and Sign Changes

When a planet is *retrograde*, it appears to be standing still momentarily from the viewpoint of an observer situated on planet Earth. Although orbiting planets never stand still, when a planet is retrograde it is as if two vehicles are moving in the same direction and one vehicle passes the other. As the faster vehicle (faster orbiting planet) passes the slower vehicle (slower orbiting planet), for a brief moment in time it appears as though the slower vehicle (slower orbiting planet) is moving backwards. Of course it is not really moving backwards, the effect is purely illusory. Sign changes are also important times to watch for when incorporating astrology into a trading strategy. As the various planets move from being in one sign to being in another, quite often one will see a short term change in trend. The following pages present numerous examples of how synodic periods, retrograde events and sign changes all impact the markets.

Mercury during Retrograde and at Sign changes

Traders should focus on those periods of time when geocentric Mercury is retrograde. During the course of a calendar year, Mercury will exhibit three retrograde periods. The chart in Figure 3-18 illustrates daily price data for the S&P continuous contract for August 2011 through to September 2012 and the Mercury retrograde events. Note that during each of these periods the markets exhibited some pronounced swings which traders could have captured using technical chart analysis. As an aside, it is interesting to note that Mercury turned retrograde exactly on the date of the 2012 US Presidential election. In traditional 'mercurial' fashion, the election yielded something of a surprise. Despite polls taken by many organizations that all showed a very tight race in the end President Obama captured a comfortable majority of electoral college votes. The day after the election, Mercury handed out yet another surprise when market indices in Europe and North America dropped hard and fast, leaving traders gasping for breath. With Mercury retrograde and also being in detriment in the sign of Sagittarius (see Table 3-1), these surprises were actually not surprises at all to those versed in astrology. For 2013 Mercury will be retrograde February 23 to March 16, June 26 to July 19 and again from October 21 to November 9.

Mercury changing signs of the Zodiac also deserves watching by traders. In particular, Mercury entering the sign of Scorpio can lead to some notable market sell-offs or some notable rallies, each of which the alert trader will be able to recognize using technical chart analysis. The chart in Figure 3-19 illustrates price action on the S&P 500 Index for the September-October 2012 period. Mercury entered the sign of Scorpio on Saturday, October 6. Note that on October 5, S&P futures made a swing high and then declined for several trading sessions. Mercury transiting through Aquarius, Pisces and part of Aries also can deliver some notable market moves which traders should be alert to. Table 3-5 presents some data going back to 2007 to further illustrate the powerful significance of Mercury changing and moving through signs of the Zodiac.

Figure 3-18 S&P 500 Index Mercury retrograde events

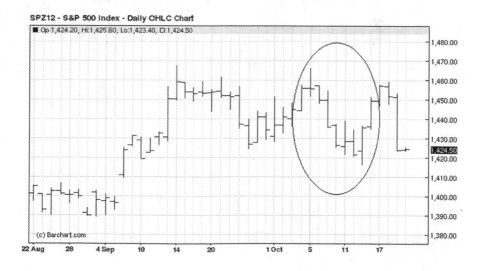

Figure 3-19 S&P 500 Index Mercury changing signs

The following Table summarizes some recent geocentric Mercury sign transits.

Event	Date(s)	Outcome
Mercury enters Scorpio	Nov 12,2007	53 point gain on S&P futures over 2 sessions
Mercury in Aquarius	Jan 9-Jan 22, 2008	261 point decline on S&P futures
Mercury through Pisces and Aries	Mar 17-April 28, 2008	146 point rally on S&P futures
Mercury enters Scorpio	Nov 5, 2008	100 point decline on S&P futures over 2 sessions
Mercury in Aquarius	Feb 15-Mar 6, 2009	75 point decline on S&P futures
Mercury through Pisces and Aries	Mar 10-Apr 28, 2009	223 point rally on S&P futures
Mercury enters Scorpio	Oct 29, 2009	37 point decline on S&P futures over 3 sessions
Mercury in Aquarius	Feb 11-Feb 22, 2010	56 point rally on S&P futures
Mercury through Pisces and Aries	Mar 2-Apr 2, 2010	66 point rally on S&P futures
Mercury enters Scorpio	Oct 21, 2010	16 point gain on S&P futures over 3 sessions
Mercury in Aquarius	Feb 4-Feb 18, 2011	44 point rally on S&P futures
Mercury through Pisces and Aries	Feb 22-May 16, 2011	62 point rally on S&P futures
Mercury enters Scorpio	Oct 13-Nov 2, 2011	100 point rally on S&P futures
Mercury in Aquarius	Jan 28-Feb15, 2012	49 point rally on S&P futures
Mercury through Pisces and Aries	Mar 6-Mar 27, 2012	82 point rally on S&P futures
Mercury in Scorpio	Oct 6-Oct 29, 2012	30 point decline followed by a 37 point rally followed by a 51 point decline on S&P futures
Mercury in Scorpio	Nov 15-Dec 11, 2012	89 point rise in S&P futures

Table 3-5 Effect on the S&P 500 Index of
Mercury changing signs

Mercury (0 degrees) Conjunction Events

Mercury conjunct Neptune (geocentric) is an aspect that traders should watch carefully for its propensity to deliver swing highs or lows to form. The chart in Figure 3-20 illustrates S&P 500 Index price action for the first 6 months of 2008. Note the four dates when Mercury was conjunct Neptune all delivered turns in trend. Although not shown on this chart, the March 2009 lows align within a couple trading sessions to a Mercury-Neptune conjunction.

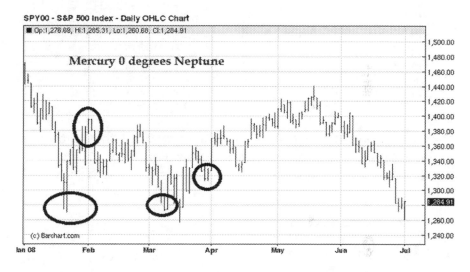

Figure 3-20 S&P 500 Index Mercury conjunct Neptune

Mercury conjunct Saturn (geocentric) is another aspect to watch for. The chart in Figure 3-21 illustrates price action for late 2009 for Alcoa (NYSE:AA). Note how the three instances of Mercury conjunct Saturn align very well with swings in price. Although not shown here, it is interesting to note that the market sell-off of early October 2011 aligns very well with a Mercury-Saturn conjunction.

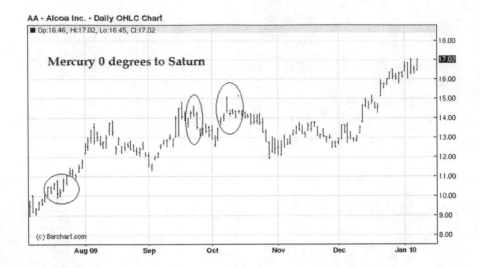

Figure 3-21 Alcoa (NYSE:AA) Mercury conjunct Saturn

Mercury conjunct Uranus (geocentric) bears watching also. The chart in Figure 3-22 illustrates S&P 500 Index price action for 2012. The three dates of conjunction shown on the chart align very well with changes in trend.

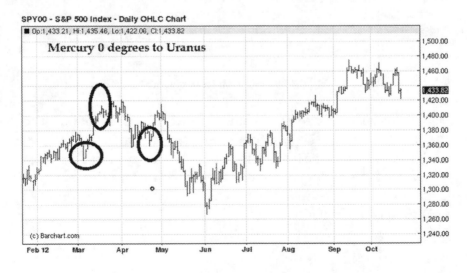

Figure 3-22 S&P 500 Index Mercury conjunct Uranus

Lastly, Mercury conjunct Mars (geocentric) is another aspect to watch for. The chart in Figure 3-23 illustrates price action for US Steel Corp in late 2010. Two of the dates of conjunction shown on the chart align with minor changes in trend while the date in February 2011 aligns with a larger degree trend change.

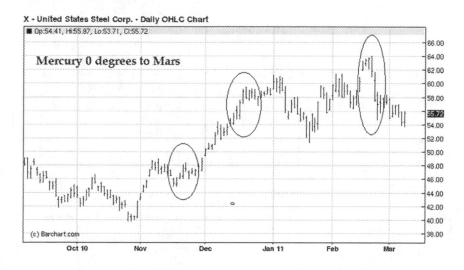

Figure 3-23 US Steel (NYSE:X) Mercury conjunct Mars

Traders and investors should be alert for significant price action on stocks when the planet Mercury is retrograde, makes sign changes or is conjunct to other planets.

Venus Retrograde Events

Earlier, I noted the importance of watching those times when Venus crosses the Mid-Heaven and Ascendant positions from the first trade chart. In addition, traders should also watch those periods of time when geocentric Venus is retrograde. Table 3-6 summarizes some of these periods going back several years. Looking forward, the next Venus retrograde event will be December 21, 2013 to January 30, 2014.

Retrograde Dates	Notes	Market Behaviour
Oct 10-Nov20, 2002	Significant market low on October 10, 2002	152 point rally on S&P futures during this retrograde period
May 17-June 28, 2004		67 point rally on S&P futures during this retrograde period
Dec 24,2005-Feb 2, 2006		48 point rally on S&P futures between December 30, 2005 and January 12, 2006
July 27-Sept 7, 2007	Significant market peak reached 1 month after retrograde event	124 point rally on S&P futures between August 16, 2007 and September 4, 2007
Mar 6-Apr 16, 2009	Significant market low on March 6, 2009	202 point rally on S&P futures during this retrograde period
Oct 8-Nov 16, 2010		79 point rally on S&P futures between October 8 and November 5, 2010
May 15-June 26, 2012	The ill-fated Facebook IPO occurred in this timeframe	93 point rally on S&P futures between June 4-20, 2012

Table 3-6 The effect of Venus retrograde events

Venus retrograde events (although not frequent) are often associated with significant market highs and lows.

Jupiter Retrograde Events and Jupiter-Sun aspects

From our vantage point here on Earth, we see Jupiter exhibit retrograde behaviour once a year or so and each of these retrograde periods lasts for about 3 ½ months. Looking back over the past decade, it becomes apparent that the market tends to exhibit only net modest changes during these retrograde periods. Only one rally of over 100 points magnitude has occurred during a Jupiter retrograde event since 2001 as Table 3-7 shows.

Retrograde Dates	S&P futures Move (close to close basis)
Nov 2, 2001-Feb 28, 2002	Gain of 17 points
Dec 3, 2002-April 2, 2003	Loss of 46 points
Jan 3, 2004-May 3, 2004	Gain of 7 points
Feb 2, 2005-June 4, 2005	Gain of 5 points
Mar 4, 2006-July 4, 2006	Gain of 11 points
Apr 6, 2007-Aug 6, 2007	Gain of 15 points
May 8, 2008-Sept 7, 2008	Loss of 125 points
June 15, 2009-Oct 11,2009	Gain of 148 points
July 22, 2010-Nov 16, 2010	Gain of 87 points
Aug 30, 2011-Dec 24, 2011	Gain of 54 points
Oct 3, 2012-Jan 29, 2013	Gain of 68 points

Table 3-7 Effect on the S&P 500 Index of
Jupiter retrograde events

From our vantage point on Earth, Jupiter can be seen to make various aspects with the Sun. It is important to examine the various aspects of Jupiter with the Sun to gain a fuller appreciation for the importance of this planet to trading strategies. The chart illustrated in Figure 3-24 shows S&P futures prices from August 2011 to August 2012. Note how the various aspects of Jupiter and Sun are closely aligned with swing highs and lows.

Figure 3-24 S&P 500 Index Jupiter-Sun aspects

Traders should watch the planet Jupiter closely, during times when it is retrograde, when it aspects the Sun or when it makes 0 degree aspects to other planets.

Jupiter conjunct Venus and Mercury events

Jupiter conjunct Venus and Mercury are geocentric events that traders should watch for. Such conjunctions only occur a few times each year. The chart in Figure 3-25 illustrates S&P 500 price action from late 2008 into 2009. The three dates circled on the chart are conjunctions of Jupiter and Mercury. Note how in the first three cases the conjunctions aligned with swing movements in the market. In the February 2009 event, the markets immediately proceeded to break down out of a sideways consolidation range.

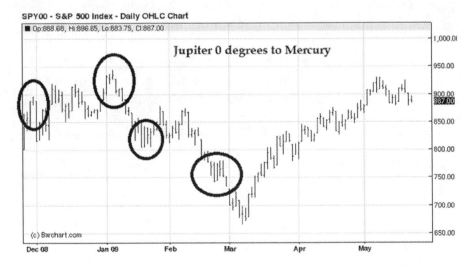

Figure 3-25 S&P 500 Index Jupiter conjunct Mercury

Conjunctions of Jupiter and Venus (geocentric) are not too common, but should be watched for regardless. The chart in Figure 3-26 shows S&P 500 price action from mid-2011 to mid-2012. During this time span, only two Jupiter-Venus conjunctions occurred. In the case of the 2011 event, price action peaked a couple trading sessions prior to a 40 point decline on the S&P. In the 2012 case, price action surged higher the session prior to the conjunction.

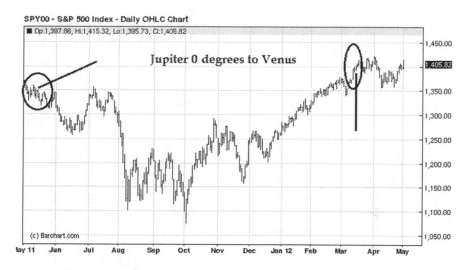

Figure 3-26 S&P 500 Index Jupiter conjunct Venus

Jupiter aspects to Mars, Saturn, Neptune and Uranus

The 90 degree square aspect between geocentric Jupiter and Mars bears close watching. An examination of the S&P futures prices dating back to 1995 shows that when Jupiter is at a 90 degree aspect to Mars one can expect to see swing tops or swing bottoms within a few days either side of the actual aspect. From February 3 to about February 16, these two planets were within orb of being 90 degrees to each other. What happened to the markets? The S&P futures peaked on February 19 and sold off for a couple trading sessions thereafter.

Another geocentric aspect to watch for is Jupiter 180 degrees to Mars. An examination of the S&P futures dating back to 1987 shows traders can expect to see swing highs or swing lows on the market on either side of this aspect.

The 0, 90 and 180 degree aspects between Jupiter and Uranus also bears watching, even though such aspects are infrequent. A review of S&P

futures dating back to 1997 shows traders can expect swing highs or swing lows at these aspects, especially if Jupiter is in the signs of Aries, Leo or Sagittarius.

A study of S&P futures data going back to 1990 shows a total of 27 geocentric aspect occurrences (0, 60, 90, 120, 180 degrees) between these Jupiter and Neptune. With one possible exception, it is evident that aspects between these planets are very closely aligned with swing highs and lows. Traders should watch for these aspects, however infrequent they may be. The chart in Figure 3-27 shows three dates in 2009 when Jupiter was conjunct Neptune.

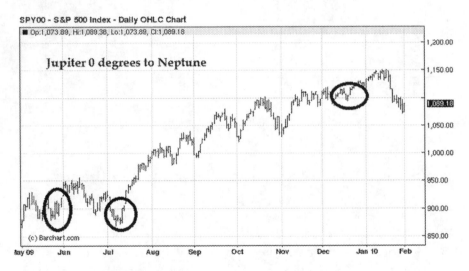

Figure 3-27 S&P 500 Index Jupiter conjunct Neptune

A study of S&P futures data going back to 1990 shows 24 aspect geocentric occurrences (0, 60, 90, 120, 180 degrees) between Jupiter and Pluto. Traders should watch carefully for these aspects to occur as they are closely aligned with swing highs and swing lows. It is also interesting to note that similar swing highs and lows can be seen when overlaying these aspects onto a chart of Crude Oil futures.

Venus conjunct either of Mars, Saturn, Neptune or Uranus

Each year there is a cluster of dates when geocentric Venus is conjunct these planets. Traders should be alert to these dates.

Figure 3-28 S&P 500 Index Venus Conjunct either of Uranus, Saturn, Neptune or Mars

Sun-Saturn events

While Saturn does have periods of retrograde activity, a study of the S&P 500 price data reveals mixed behaviour. What is more important are those times when geocentric Saturn makes various aspects of with the Sun. Figure 3-29 illustrates price action of the S&P 500 Index for 12 months starting from September 2011. Note how aspect angles 22.5, 45, 60, 90, 135 and 150 all can align very well with swing highs and lows. When applying Sun-Saturn aspects to other stocks, ETF's or commodity contracts traders should look at all the various aspects to see if any stand out as being more powerful than others.

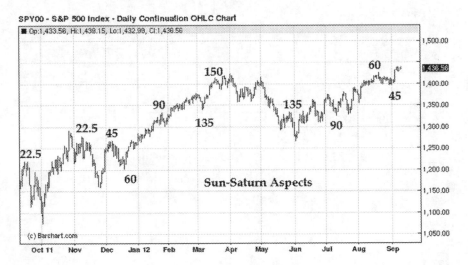

Figure 3-29 S&P 500 Index Saturn-Sun aspects

Traders and investors should watch for Sun-Saturn events to correlate with price swings on major market indices such as the Dow Jones, the S&P 500 and the Toronto Stock Exchange.

Saturn conjunct Mercury events

Saturn conjunct Mercury (geocentric) events are not very frequent, but do deserve watching. The chart in Figure 3-30 illustrates three such events in 2009. The first two align very well with pivotal turns on price action, the third with only a small interruption in trend. It is further interesting to note the market lows in October 2011 align within a few trading sessions to the bottom registered in that month.

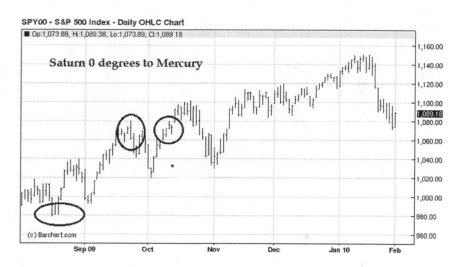

Figure 3-30 S&P 500 Index Saturn conjunct Mercury

Mars-Uranus events

A study of S&P futures performance dating back to 2000 has shown that traders should carefully study the various geocentric aspects of Mars and Uranus. The correlation of their aspects to swing highs and swing lows is very strong indeed. For 2013, there will be nine various aspects to watch for.

Sun conjunct Uranus combination in aspect to Jupiter

The geocentric combination of Sun conjunct Uranus in aspect to Jupiter deserves to be pencilled in on longer term trading calendars. When Sun and Uranus are at a 0 degree separation to each other, which is a yearly event, watch for those instances when the planet Jupiter then makes a 0, 30, 60, 90, 120 or 180 degree aspect to this conjunct pair. A study of S&P futures data going back to 1990 shows that these aspect occurrences are closely associated with swing highs or lows. A notable example of such occurred in March of 2009 within days of a major low when Jupiter was 180 degrees opposite to the conjunct Sun-Uranus pair. The end of March 2013 will see a Sun-Uranus 0 degree aspect with Jupiter at 60 degrees to this pair.

Saturn-Uranus events

Geocentric Saturn and Uranus aspects in the context of technology stocks makes for an interesting study. A look at Nasdaq futures data going back to 1999 shows that the 14 aspect events between these two planets are closely aligned with swing highs or lows. In fact, the ultimate top on Nasdaq occurred when these two planets were within 5 degrees of registering an exact 90 degree hard aspect to one another. Traders of technology stocks should watch all aspects between these two bodies for possible turning points on Nasdaq and technology stocks.

Neptune through the Signs

Planet Neptune orbits the Sun is just over 163 years, spending just under 14 years in each Zodiac sign. A study of historic data has shown that the times when geocentric Neptune changes signs are all too often times of trend change on the markets as was the case in early 1970, early 1984 and early 1998. The most recent sign change occurred in early April 2011 shortly after which S&P futures reached a peak that remained unchallenged for 10 months.

Uranus through the Signs

Uranus changing signs of the zodiac is an infrequent occurrence, but one that nonetheless deserves watching. An examination of historical data of the Dow Jones Industrial average reveals that geocentric Uranus sign changes in September 1968, September 1975, November 1981 and March 2011 were all closely associated (within several weeks either side of the actual date) with swing highs on the market.

Other aspect events to be alert for include Saturn conjunct Mercury, Mars-Uranus, Sun-Uranus with Jupiter, Sun-Uranus, Neptune changing signs and Uranus changing signs.

Aspects between planets, first trade dates and synodic periods comprise some heavy subject matter. Incorporating these techniques into an overall trading strategy may at first seem daunting. However, with repeated practice, it soon becomes very straightforward. Let's now turn our attention to an exploration of how astrology can be used as part of a trading strategy for commodity futures.

CHAPTER FOUR

Astrology and Commodity Futures

So far in this book the focus has been mainly on geocentric astrology in which the vantage point for determining planetary phenomena is the Earth. The *New American Ephemeris for the 21st Century* referred to earlier is based on geocentric astrology. Heliocentric astrology sometimes appears in older writings related to trading the commodity futures markets. Recall that in heliocentric astrology there are no house divisions, no Ascendant, Mid-Heaven or retrograde motions. Planetary aspects and sign changes are determined with a vantage point being the Sun. This seemingly simplified approach may well explain the decline in its popularity amongst astrologers. Even though the heliocentric approach may no longer be as popular, its effectiveness as a tool to assist traders and investors has not diminished.

As mentioned in the previous chapter, heliocentric astrology requires the use of an ephemeris containing heliocentric data. In the absence of such an ephemeris, a good venue for obtaining heliocentric data is the website **www.astro.com/swisseph/swepha_e.htm.** If you are using a software program to generate first trade charts, select the heliocentric format when entering the parameters to create the chart.

What follows in this chapter is a look at several commodity futures contracts where price action aligns very well with astrologic phenomena—some of it geocentric, some of it heliocentric. It must be stressed that when trading commodity futures, all the astrological techniques and phenomena discussed in this book up to this point will also apply. The examples that follow show certain additional aspects and phenomena that older literature sources have suggested apply to commodity futures. As a note of caution, trading on the futures markets entails much more risk than on the equity markets due to the use of leverage. Being aware of the larger degree prevailing trend is vitally important when trading commodity futures.

Gold futures

Gold futures started trading on the New York Mercantile Exchange on December 31, 1974.

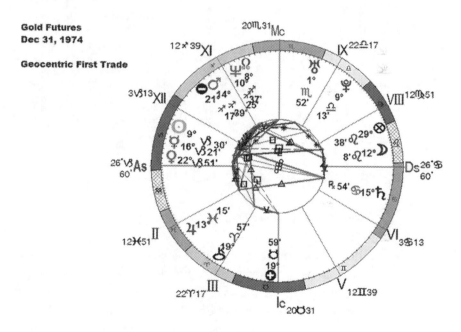

Figure 4-1 Gold futures geocentric first trade chart

Figure 4-1 shows the first trade date chart for Gold futures in geocentric format. Notice how Pluto and Sun are 90 degrees aspect to one another. Note also how the North Node is at a 30 degree aspect to the Sun. Lastly, Venus is on the Ascendant which bodes well for some repetitive patterns.

The daily chart in Figure 4-2 shows Gold price action for 12 months starting October 2011. The un-shaded arrows drawn on the chart show the Sun-Pluto 0, 60, 90, 120 and 180 degree aspects. The shaded arrows show the Sun-North Node 0, 60, 90, 120 and 180 degree aspects. Note how these aspect dates align very well with short term trend turning points. While there remain many other swing bottoms and tops on the chart, the Sun-Pluto and Sun-North Node aspects align with enough occurrences to make a significant difference to the success of a trader who follows Gold futures.

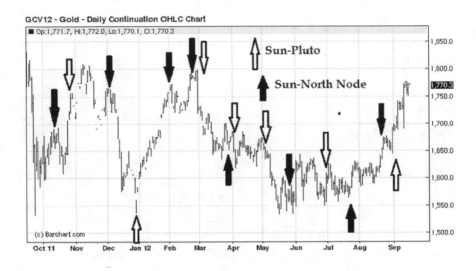

Figure 4-2 Aspects affecting Gold futures prices

Neptune and Pluto also align very closely to Gold swing highs and swing lows at times of moving from being Retrograde to being Direct again. The weekly chart in Figure 4-3 shows Gold futures prices going back to 2008 and illustrates those periods when Pluto was retrograde. Notice that Pluto will be retrograde once a year. Observe that immediately after each retrograde event Gold prices register a swing high or low of varying magnitude.

Figure 4-3 Pluto retrograde events and Gold futures prices

The chart in Figure 4-4 is similar to that in Figure 4-3, except that it illustrates the times when Neptune is retrograde. Notice that at the conclusion of each Neptune retrograde event, Gold prices register a swing high or low of varying magnitude.

Figure 4-4 Neptune retrograde events and Gold futures prices

Whether you are trading Gold futures or investing in Gold mining equities, pay particular attention to geocentric Sun-Pluto and Sun-North Node aspects. Also watch carefully those times when Pluto and Neptune go from being retrograde to being direct.

Silver futures

The first trade date for Silver futures was July 5, 1933. The first trade chart using geocentric format is displayed in Figure 4-5. Note the Sun and Moon are nearly opposite to each other thus suggesting that these two bodies will figure prominently in Silver price swings.

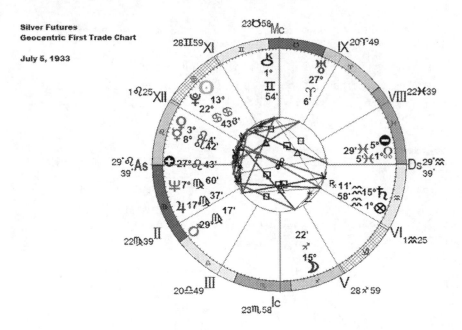

Figure 4-5 Silver futures first trade chart

The chart in Figure 4-6 illustrates daily-nearest Silver futures prices during 2012. Un-shaded arrows depict Full Moons and shaded arrows are New Moons. Notice how these Moon phase events align closely with swing highs, swing lows and break-outs. The other phenomenon to note is the position of the Sun at 13 degrees Cancer in the Silver first trade chart.

Zero degrees of Cancer each year marks the Summer Solstice. Hence, Silver futures started trading a mere two weeks after the solstice which means that the time around annual solstice and equinox events may play a role in Silver price fluctuations.

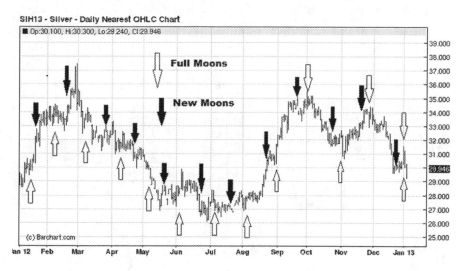

Figure 4-6 Lunar events affecting Silver futures prices

Whether you are trading Silver futures or investing in pure-play Silver mining equities, pay particular attention to Moon phases and times surrounding the annual equinoxes and solstices.

Copper futures

The first trade date for Copper futures was July 29, 1988. The geocentric chart shows that at the time Copper futures started trading, Sun and Mercury were 0 degrees apart and there was a lunar eclipse event going on as well. The chart in Figure 4-7 shows Copper futures prices going back to late 2011. Note how the Sun-Mercury conjunct events align very closely to price swings as well as price breakdowns and breakouts. This chart also shows two lunar eclipse events. Again note how these align with significant turning points in price.

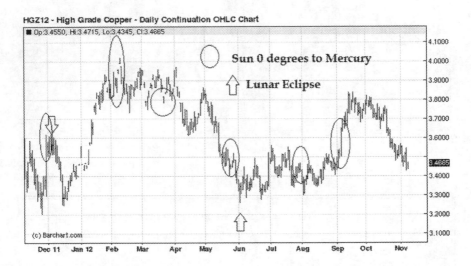

Figure 4-7 Aspects affecting Copper futures prices

Whether you are trading Copper futures or investing in pure-play Copper mining equities, pay particular attention to geocentric Sun-Mercury conjunct aspects as well as eclipse events.

Crude Oil futures

Crude Oil futures started trading in New York on March 3, 1983. The first trade chart in geocentric format shows that Pluto is on the Descendant line and Sun-Neptune aspect each other at a 72 degree angle which is a unique aspect as 72 degrees is $1/5^{th}$ of 360 degrees. This likely explains why older writings on financial astrology dating back over 25 years indicate that Sun-Pluto and Sun-Neptune aspects should be watched closely when trading Crude Oil futures. In Figure 4-8, the circled timeframes are those in which a Sun-Pluto aspect occurred followed within days by a Sun-Neptune aspect. Notice the distinct volatility during these aspects that an alert trader could take advantage of.

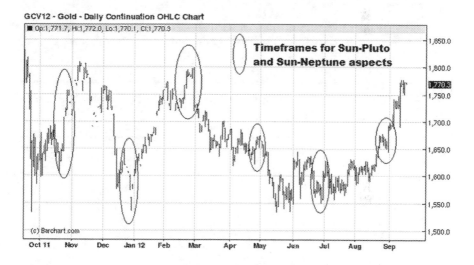

Figure 4-8 Aspects affecting Crude Oil futures prices

Old writings by Long and others mention Pluto and Neptune retrograde. Figure 4-9 illustrates weekly price action on Crude Oil futures dating from November 2010 to present. Notice how the periods of Pluto and Neptune going retrograde are associated with significant price highs or lows.

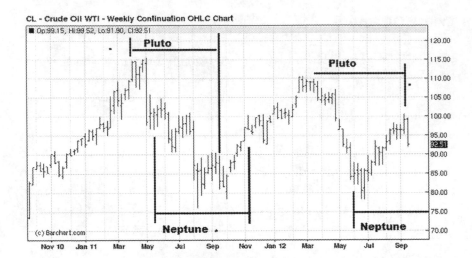

Figure 4-9 Crude Oil futures prices and Pluto-Neptune aspects

Energy market followers should watch for price trend swings on Crude Oil to align with geocentric Sun-Pluto and Sun-Neptune events.

Wheat, Corn and Oats futures

Wheat futures (as well as Corn and Oats futures) started trading in Chicago on January 2, 1877. Figure 4-10 shows the heliocentric first trade chart. Observations that immediately can be seen are Mercury and Jupiter in a 90 degree square aspect to each other, Mercury and Saturn nine degrees apart for a conjunction and also a Venus-Mars conjunction. Financial astrology books from the 1970s suggest that Mercury-Jupiter and Mercury-Saturn aspects are key to following price swings on Wheat, Corn and Oats.

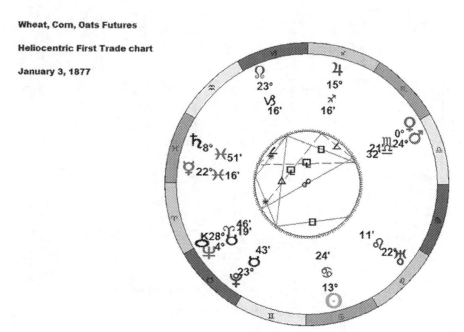

Wheat, Corn, Oats Futures

Heliocentric First Trade chart

January 3, 1877

Figure 4-10 Wheat, Corn, Oats heliocentric first trade chart

Traders of Wheat, Corn and Oats futures should pay particular attention to heliocentric aspects of Mercury-Jupiter and Mercury-Saturn. Heliocentric Mercury changing signs can also play a role in price swings. Geocentric Mars square Moon also holds potential for price swings on Corn futures.

Figure 4-11 illustrates a daily continuation chart for Wheat futures dating from October 2011. Overlaid on this chart are the 0, 90 and 180 degree aspects between heliocentric Mercury and Saturn shown as shaded dots. The shaded arrows are the 0, 90 and 180 degree aspects between heliocentric Mercury and Jupiter. There are many factors that determine grain futures prices including weather and government agency reports. But, nevertheless, Figure 4-11 does show that the Mercury-Saturn and Mercury-Jupiter aspects do align reasonably well enough with price swings. Traders of grain futures would be wise to watch for these aspects to occur.

Figure 4-11 Wheat futures prices and heliocentric
Mercury-Saturn aspects

The financial astrology writings of Jeanne Long suggest that Wheat traders should also watch dates when heliocentric Mercury changes signs. Figure 4-12 illustrates the time frame of August 22-28, 2012. Using this hourly chart, an alert trader could have caught the move when Mercury moved into Gemini. On August 28, 2012 a downtrend ended when Mercury entered Cancer.

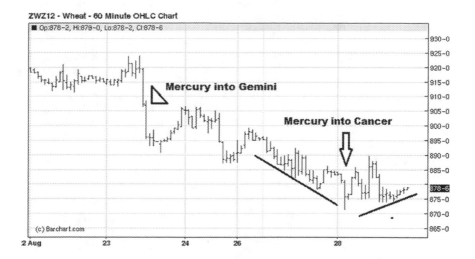

Figure 4-12 Wheat futures prices and heliocentric
Mercury changing signs

As for Corn futures, Figure 4-13 shows daily continuation price action of Corn futures dating from October 2011. The arrows are the dates of 0 and 180 degree aspects of heliocentric Mercury and Saturn. The shaded dots are dates of 0, 90 and 180 degree aspects of Mercury and Jupiter. Again there are many factors than can lead to swings in Corn prices, but the correlation of price swings to these heliocentric aspects is a unique tool that a trader can add to his or her arsenal of techniques. As noted above, heliocentric Mercury changing signs aligns to swings in Wheat prices. Although not shown here, there are also well-documented techniques that call for Corn traders to watch for heliocentric Mercury changing signs and for geocentric Mars to be square the Moon. Heliocentric Mercury will change signs approximately once every six days. Such dates that fall during the Monday to Friday trading week should be watched in particular. Geocentric Mars will be at a 90 degree aspect to Moon approximately two times each month.

Figure 4-13 Corn futures prices and heliocentric
Mercury-Saturn aspects

Soybean futures

Soybean futures started trading in Chicago on October 5, 1936. Old financial astrology literature by Pesavento and others states that traders should watch heliocentric Venus as it changes signs. How this empirical notion was arrived at may be in part related to the heliocentric first trade chart alignment of Venus with Mercury and Neptune. Note that Venus is 90 degrees (square) to Neptune. Venus is further 135 degrees to Mercury. Neptune is also 135 degrees to Mercury. This configuration is called *Thor's Hammer* by astrologers. Old literature also states that Soybean traders should be alert to those times when geocentric Mercury turns direct after being in retrograde. Figure 4-14 illustrates the heliocentric first trade chart of Soybean futures.

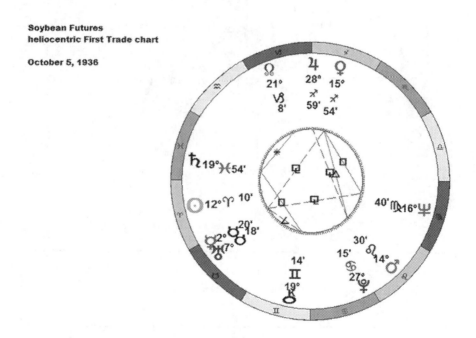

Figure 4-14 Soybean futures heliocentric first trade chart

The chart in Figure 4-15 displays Soybean futures price action for the latter part of 2012. The arrows point to those times when heliocentric Venus changed signs. Note the close correlation to changes in trend. Some of these trend changes were minor and best suited to short term trading. However, the Venus sign change in in mid-August led to a sizeable rally to the upside. The sign change at the end of August was the start of a larger sell-off. The sign change in mid-November was the start of a move up and the sign change in early December was closely aligned to the start of a nasty year-end move to the downside. Geocentric Mercury going from retrograde back to direct as it did in early August and again in late November can also be seen to correlate well to trend changes. Again, there are many factors that affect the Soybean trade including weather and export data, but Venus sign changes and Mercury turning direct seem to correlate all too well for a trader to ignore.

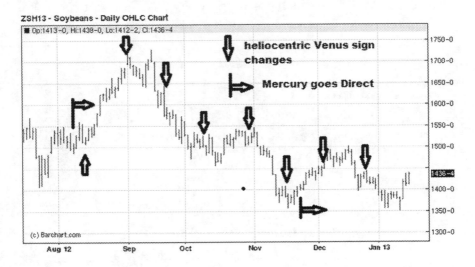

Figure 4-15 Aspects affecting Soybean futures prices

Soybean futures traders should watch for heliocentric Venus to change signs. Geocentric Mercury going from retrograde back to direct also holds potential for price swings.

Soybean Oil futures

Soybean Oil futures started trading on July 17, 1950. The heliocentric version of the first trade chart shows Mercury within a few degrees of being conjunct to Pluto. Figure 4-16 shows price action of Soybean Oil futures for the 12 months commencing in late 2011. On the chart, note the occurrences of heliocentric Mercury being 0 degrees to Pluto. Although not shown on this chart, traders also should take careful note of those dates when heliocentric Mercury changes signs of the Zodiac. Such sign changes occur three to five times a month.

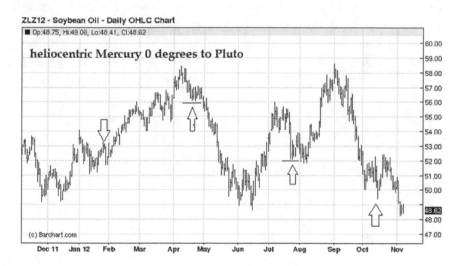

Figure 4-16 Aspects affecting Soybean Oil futures prices

Soybean Meal futures

Soybean Meal started trading August 9, 1951. The heliocentric version of the first trade chart shows that Venus had just changed signs, entering Aquarius, thus providing a strong hint that Venus changing signs might figure in price swings for the futures contract. Also evident on the heliocentric first trade chart is a conjunction between Mercury and asteroid body Chiron which is situated between Saturn and Uranus. Chiron has an orbital period of about 50 years and although not often mentioned in financial astrology, is important nonetheless. The chart in Figure 4-17 shows price action for Soybean Meal for the six months following May 2012. Note how the times corresponding to sign changes align very well with price swings. Note also that those times when heliocentric Mercury is 0, 90, or 180 degrees to Chiron seem to also align very well.

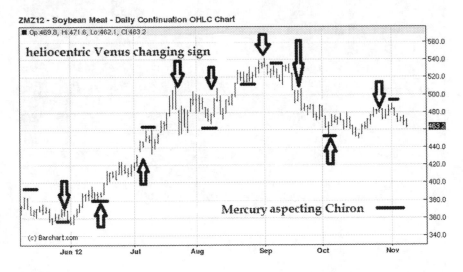

Figure 4-17 Aspects affecting Soybean Meal futures prices

Traders of Soybean Meal futures should watch carefully for heliocentric Venus to change signs and for heliocentric Mercury to aspect asteroid body Chiron. Traders of Soybean Oil futures should watch carefully for heliocentric Mercury to change signs. Trend shifts also may be correlated to heliocentric Mercury being 0 degrees to Pluto.

Canadian Dollar and British Pound

Aspects between heliocentric Mercury and Saturn play a role in the price swings on Currency futures.

The chart in Figure 4-18 shows Canadian Dollar futures price action for 1 year starting from mid-September 2011. Canadian Dollar futures and British Pound futures both began trading on the Chicago Mercantile Exchange on May 16, 1972.

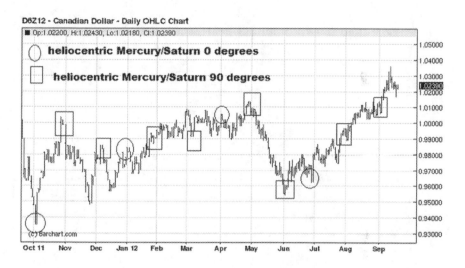

Figure 4-18 Canadian Dollar and British Pound
heliocentric first trade chart

In Figure 4-18, the timeframes associated with a 0 degree aspect between heliocentric Mercury and Saturn are denoted by a circle. The timeframes associated with a 90 degree aspect are denoted by a square. Note the close correlation between price trend changes and these Mercury-Saturn aspects. Knowing that a heliocentric Mercury-Saturn aspect is approaching, Canadian dollar and British Pound currency traders can use shorter term charts to watch for a suitable trade entry points.

The 30 minute chart in Figure 4-19 illustrates price action for British pound futures on August 31, 2012. On this date, heliocentric Mercury was at a 90 degree aspect to heliocentric Saturn. Note the rise of 100 points on the futures, a gain of $625 for the alert trader on a single contract.

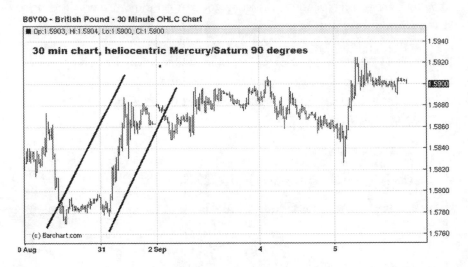

Figure 4-19 British Pound futures 30 minute chart

Currency futures traders should be alert for heliocentric Mercury-Saturn aspects to influence the British Pound and the Canadian Dollar.

Japanese Yen

The Japanese Yen also responds well to astrological aspects.Traders for many years have been following the heliocentric Mercury-Pluto aspects. Figure 4-20 displays Yen futures price action with the 0, 90 and 180 degree heliocentric Mercury-Pluto aspects denoted by circled timeframes. Note the strong correlation to swing highs and lows. While the Mercury-Pluto aspects do not account for every pivotal swing in price, the correlation is strong enough that traders of Yen currency futures would be wise to watch closely for these Mercury-Pluto aspects to occur.

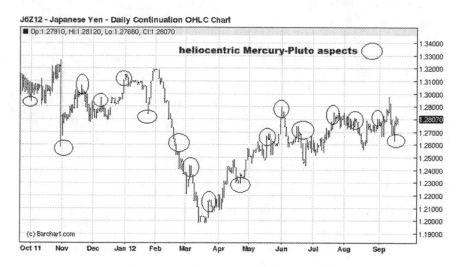

Figure 4-20 Aspects affecting Japanese Yen futures prices

Heliocentric Mercury-Pluto aspects can influence the Japanese Yen. Futures traders should be alert for these aspects to occur.

Euro

The heliocentric first trade chart for the Euro which became the official currency for the European Union on January 1, 2002 shows a clear connection of 120 degrees (trine) between Mercury and Jupiter. The chart in Figure 4-21 presents futures price action for the period December 2011 to November 2012. Note the various occurrences of heliocentric Mercury trine Jupiter and how they align very closely with swings in price.

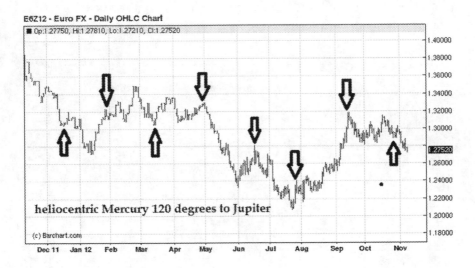

Figure 4-21 Aspects affecting Euro futures prices

Heliocentric aspects that have Mercury 120 degrees to Jupiter are often associated with trend swings on the Euro currency.

Australian Dollar

The geocentric first trade chart for the Australian Dollar futures which started trading in Chicago on January 13, 1987 clearly shows Sun and Mercury conjunct (0 degrees) in the sign of Capricorn. The chart in Figure 4-22 presents futures price action for the period December 2011 to November 2012. Note the various occurrences of geocentric Mercury conjunct Sun and how they align very closely with swings in price.

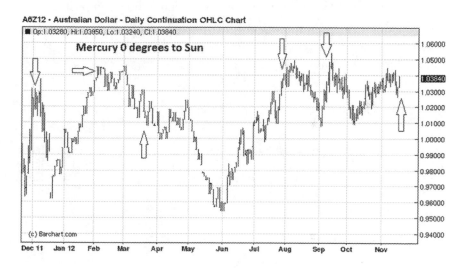

Figure 4-22 Aspects affecting Aussie Dollar futures prices

Geocentric occurrences of Mercury 0 degrees to Sun often align with trend changes on the Australian dollar.

Live Cattle

Live Cattle futures first started trading on the Chicago Mercantile exchange on November 30, 1964. The chart in Figure 4-23 shows weekly price action dating back to 2008. Notice how Live Cattle futures exhibit either swings in trend and also sharp moves in price around the times corresponding to 180 days and 360 days from November 30. Note also how periods of Mars being retrograde are associated with significant price levels. The Mars retrograde event in late 2009 represented the lowest price level for Live Cattle futures between 2008 and late 2012. The Mars retrograde event of 2012 represented the highest price noted during this time frame. Clearly, Mars retrograde events should be taken very seriously by Cattle futures traders.

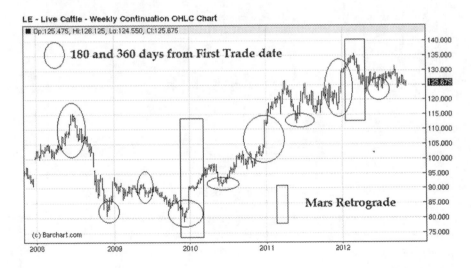

Figure 4-23 Aspects affecting Live Cattle futures prices

Traders of Live Cattle futures should be alert to times when Mars turns retrograde.

Lean Hogs

Lean Hog futures started trading on February 28, 1966 on the Chicago Mercantile Exchange. The chart in Figure 4-24 illustrates price action on a weekly basis dating back to 2008. If using geocentric astrology to follow Hog futures, note how the North Node of Moon changing sign is closely aligned with significant price swings. The heliocentric first trade chart for Lean Hogs shows that Sun is 90 degrees square to Mercury. The heliocentric squaring of these two bodies occurs six or seven times each year and these dates are indicated on the chart in Figure 4-24 as well. Notice how these dates all too often occur in very close proximity to swings in price.

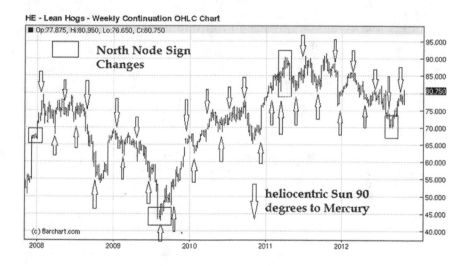

Figure 4-24 Aspects affecting Lean Hogs futures prices

Traders of Lean Hog futures should watch for North Node sign changes. On a shorter term basis, heliocentric Mercury making 90 degree aspects to Sun is also important.

Lumber

Lumber futures started trading in Chicago on October 1, 1969. The chart in Figure 4-25 illustrates price action on a weekly basis for Lumber futures going back to 2008. Note how the occurrences of heliocentric Mercury being 180 degrees opposite Jupiter align very closely with swings in price. In fact, on the heliocentric first trade chart for Lumber futures, Mercury is within two degrees of being opposite Jupiter.

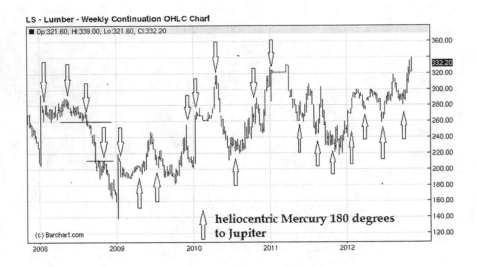

Figure 4-25 Aspects affecting Lumber futures prices

Lumber futures traders should watch for heliocentric Jupiter to make 180 degree aspects to Mercury.

30 Year Bonds

The geocentric first Trade chart of 30 Year Treasury Bond futures is a most interesting one indeed as Figure 4-26 shows. Mars is within two weeks of changing sign, is about to aspect Jupiter, is 30 degrees to Venus, is within orb of being 60 degrees to Sun and Saturn and is 90 degrees to Mercury. Financial astrology writings by Pesavento researched while preparing this book spoke very strongly in favour of watching those times when Mars was changing sign and when it was making notable aspects with other planets. Judging from the first trade chart, this now makes sense. Figure 4-27 illustrates price action on Bond futures dating back five years. Notice how the times when Mars changes sign align very well with significant price trend changes. Note also how the periods of Mars being retrograde align closely with some significant turning points in price.

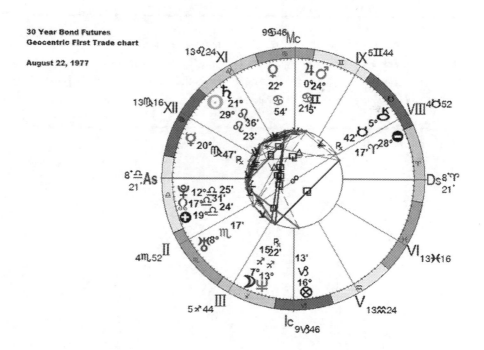

Figure 4-26 30 Year Bond futures geocentric first trade chart

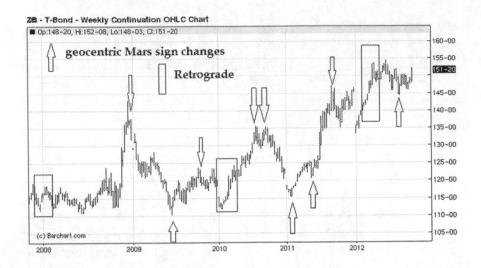

Figure 4-27 Aspects affecting 30 Year Bond futures prices

Bond futures traders should be alert to those times when geocentric Mars changes signs and also when geocentric Mars turns retrograde. The challenging factor at this time however continues to be the persistent intervention of the Federal Reserve into the bond markets which can derail astrological effects.

Epilogue

Final Thoughts

The financial markets are a dynamic entity fueled by many factors, some of which we can easily comprehend, some of which are esoteric. Astrological phenomena can drive price action and create trend changes across both short and longer term time horizons. This book has introduced you to an extensive range of astrological phenomena and shown you numerous examples to illustrate how these phenomena impact various markets. With the information gleaned from this book, I sincerely hope you will now feel compelled to make astrology a companion to technical chart analysis as you trade the markets. I further hope that as you do so, you will come to view the financial markets in a very different way.

Appendix A

New Moon and Full Moon Data for 2013 and 2014

2013 Date	New Moon	Full Moon	2014 Date	New Moon	Full Moon
January 11	X		January 1	X	
January 27		X	January 16	.	X
February 10	X		January 30	X	
February 25		X	February 14		X
March 11	X		March 1	X	
March 27		X	March 16		X
April 10	X		March 30	X	
April 25 (L)		X	April 15 (L)		X
May 10 (S)	X		April 29 (S)	X	
May 25 (L)		X	May 14		X
June 8	X		May 28	X	
June 23		X	June 13		X
July 8	X		June 27	X	
July 22		X	July 12		X
August 6	X		July 26	X	
August 21		X	August 10		X
September 5	X		August 25	X	
September 19		X	September 9		X
October 5	X		September 24	X	
October 18 (L)		X	October 8 (L)		X
November 3 (S)	X		October 23 (S)	X	
November 17		X	November 6		X
December 3	X		November 22	X	
December 17		X	December 6		X
			December 22	X	

(S) Solar eclipse (L) Lunar eclipse

2013 Perigee and Apogee Dates

2013 Perigee Date	2013 Apogee Date
January 10	January 22
February 7	February 19
March 5	March 19
March 31	April 15
April 27	May 13
May 26	June 9
June 23	July 7
July 21	August 3
August 19	August 30
September 15	September 27
October 10	October 25
November 6	November 22
December 4	December 19

2014 Perigee and Apogee Dates

2014 Perigee Date	2014 Apogee Date
January 1	January 16
January 30	February 19
February 27	March 19
March 27	April 15
April 23	May 13
May 18	June 9
June 15	July 7
July 13	August 3
August 20	August 30
September 8	September 27
October 6	October 25
November 3	November 22
November 27	December 19
December 24	

Table A-3

Appendix B

Retrograde Events 2013 and 2014

2013 Planetary Retrograde Events

Mercury Retrograde: February 23-March 16, June 26-July 19, October 21-November 9

Venus Retrograde: December 21-January 30,2014

Jupiter Retrograde: October 4, 2012-January 29, 2013, November 7,2013-March 5, 2014

Saturn Retrograde: February 18, 2013-July 7, 2013

Uranus Retrograde: July 17-December 16, 2013

Pluto Retrograde: April 12-September 19, 2013

2014 Planetary Retrograde Events

Mercury Retrograde: February 6-February 27, June 7-July 1, October 4-October 24

Venus Retrograde: December 21, 2013-January 30,2014

Jupiter Retrograde: November 7,2013-March 5, 2014, December 8-April 6, 2015

Saturn Retrograde: March 2, 2014-July 19, 2014

Uranus Retrograde: July 22-December 20, 2014

Pluto Retrograde: April 14-September 22, 2014

Appendix C

Sun-Planet Aspects

2013 Sun-Jupiter Aspects

2013 Date	Aspect
January 25	120 degrees
February 25	90 degrees
April 1	60 degrees
April 20	45 degrees
May 9	30 degrees
June 19	0 degrees
July 30	30 degrees
August 19	45 degrees
September 7	60 degrees
October 12	90 degrees
November 12	120 degrees

2014 Sun-Jupiter Aspects

2013 Date	Aspect
January 5	180 degrees
February 28	120 degrees
April 1	90 degrees
May 6	60 degrees
May 25	45 degrees
June 13	30 degrees
July 24	0 degrees
September 3	30 degrees
September 22	45 degrees
October 10	60 degrees
November 13	90 degrees
December 14	120 degrees

2013 Sun-Saturn Aspects

2013 Date	Aspect
March 1	120 degrees
April 28	180 degrees
June 26	120 degrees
July 27	90 degrees
August 30	60 degrees
September 16	45 degrees
October 3	30 degrees
November 6	0 degrees
December 9	30 degrees
December 26	45 degrees

2014 Sun-Saturn Aspects

2014 Date	Aspect
January 11	60 degrees
February 11	90 degrees
March 13	120 degrees
May 10	180 degrees
July 8	120 degrees
August 9	90 degrees
September 11	60 degrees
September 28	45 degrees
October 15	30 degrees

2013 Sun-Pluto Aspects

2013 Date	Aspect
January 29	30 degrees
February 14	45 degrees
March 1	60 degrees
March 31	90 degrees
May 1	120 degrees
July 1	180 degrees
September 1	120 degrees
October 1	90 degrees
November 1	60 degrees
November 16	45 degrees
December 2	30 degrees

2014 Sun-Pluto Aspects

2014 Date	Aspect
January 1	0 degrees
February 13	0 degrees
February 16	45 degrees
March 3	90 degrees
May 3	120 degrees
July 4	180 degrees
September 3	120 degrees
October 4	90 degrees
November 3	60 degrees
November 19	45 degrees
December 4	30 degrees

2013 Sun-Venus Aspects

2013 Date	Aspect
March 28	0 degrees
July 21	30 degrees
October 4	45 degrees
November 22	45 degrees
December 20	30 degrees

2014 Sun-Venus Aspects

2014 Date	Aspect
January 11	0 degrees
February 2	30 degrees
March 4	45 degrees
April 15	45 degrees
July 1	30 degrees
October 25	0 degrees

2013 Sun-Mercury Aspects

2013 Date	Aspect
January 18	0 degrees
March 4	0 degrees
May 11	0 degrees
July 9	0 degrees
August 24	0 degrees
November 1	0 degrees
December 29	0 degrees

2014 Sun-Mercury Aspects

2014 Date	Aspect
February 15	0 degrees
April 25	0 degrees
June 19	0 degrees
August 8	0 degrees
October 16	0 degrees
December 8	0 degrees

2013 Sun-North Node Aspects

2013 Date	Aspect
January 12	60 degrees
February 9	90 degrees
March 10	120 degrees
May 7	180 degrees
July 5	120 degrees
August 4	90 degrees
September 2	60 degrees
September 17	45 degrees
October 1	30 degrees
October 30	0 degrees
November 27	30 degrees
December 12	45 degrees
December 26	60 degrees

2014 Sun-North Node Aspects

2014 Date	Aspect
January 23	90 degrees
February 20	120 degrees
April 18	180 degrees
June 16	120 degrees
July 16	90 degrees
August 15	60 degrees
August 29	45 degrees
September 13	30 degrees
October 12	0 degrees
November 10	30 degrees
November 24	45 degrees
December 8	60 degrees

2013 Sun-Neptune Aspects

2013 Date	Aspect
January 6	45 degrees
January 21	30 degrees
February 21	0 degrees
March 24	30 degrees
April 8	60 degrees
May 26	90 degrees
June 26	120 degrees
August 26	180 degrees
October 25	120 degrees
November 24	90 degrees
December 24	60 degrees

2014 Sun-Neptune Aspects

2014 Date	Aspect
January 8	45 degrees
January 23	30 degrees
February 23	0 degrees
March 26	30 degrees
April 11	45 degrees
April 27	60 degrees
May 28	90 degrees
June 29	120 degrees
August 29	180 degrees
October 28	120 degrees
November 27	90 degrees
December 26	60 degrees

Appendix D

2013 Mercury-Jupiter Aspects

2013 Date	Aspect
January 22	120 degrees
February 9	90 degrees
March 9	90 degrees
March 29	90 degrees
April 23	60 degrees
May 2	45 degrees
May 10	30 degrees
May 27	0 degrees
August 14	30 degrees
August 22	45 degrees
August 30	60 degrees
September 19	90 degrees
November 28	120 degrees

2014 Mercury-Jupiter Aspects

2014 Date	Aspect
January 3	180 degrees
March 26	120 degrees
April 14	90 degrees
April 30	60 degrees
May 8	45 degrees
May 17	30 degrees
June 25	30 degrees
July 12	30 degrees
August 2	0 degrees
August 19	30 degrees
August 29	45 degrees
September 10	60 degrees
October 20	60 degrees
November 1	60 degrees
November 23	90 degrees
December 12	120 degrees

2013 Mercury-Saturn Aspects

2013 Date	Aspect
January 6	60 degrees
January 25	90 degrees
February 12	120 degrees
March 7	120 degrees
March 28	120 degrees
May 5	180 degrees
June 3	120 degrees
August 11	90 degrees
August 27	60 degrees
September 4	45 degrees
September 14	30 degrees
October 8	0 degrees
October 29	0 degrees
November 25	0 degrees
December 17	30 degrees
December 27	45 degrees

2014 Mercury-Saturn Aspects

2014 Date	Aspect
January 6	60 degrees
January 25	90 degrees
February 19	90 degrees
March 11	90 degrees
April 2	120 degrees
May 2	180 degrees
July 24	120 degrees
August 8	90 degrees
August 25	60 degrees
September 4	45 degrees
September 16	30 degrees
October 17	30 degrees
November 4	30 degrees
November 25	0 degrees
December 16	30 degrees
December 26	45 degrees

2013 Mercury-Pluto Aspects

2013 Date	Aspect
January 6	0 degrees
February 2	45 degrees
February 12	60 degrees
March 7	60 degrees
March 29	60 degrees
April 21	90 degrees
May 7	120 degrees
June 7	180 degrees
August 28	120 degrees
September 14	90 degrees
October 6	60 degrees
November 1	60 degrees
November 20	60 degrees
December 1	45 degrees
December 11	30 degrees
December 31	0 degrees

2014 Mercury-Pluto Aspects

2014 Date	Aspect
January 18	30 degrees
January 28	45 degrees
February 15	45 degrees
March 16	45 degrees
March 28	60 degrees
April 15	90 degrees
April 29	120 degrees
July 22	180 degrees
August 21	120 degrees
September 9	90 degrees
November 16	60 degrees
November 26	45 degrees
December 5	30 degrees
December 25	0 degrees

2013 Mercury-Venus Aspects

2013 Date	Aspect
March 7	0 degrees
May 24	0 degrees
July 11	30 degrees
July 20	45 degrees
August 16	45 degrees
September 4	30 degrees
October 24	30 degrees
October 31	45 degrees
November 8	60 degrees
November 27	60 degrees
December 13	45 degrees
December 23	30 degrees

2014 Mercury-Venus Aspects

2014 Date	Aspect
January 7	0 degrees
January 21	30 degrees
January 30	45 degrees
February 11	45 degrees
February 21	30 degrees
April 10	30 degrees
April 27	45 degrees
May 15	60 degrees
May 28	60 degrees
June 12	45 degrees
June 21	30 degrees
August 22	30 degrees
October 1	30 degrees
October 17	0 degrees

2013 Mercury-Mars Aspects

2013 Date	Aspect
January 6	30 degrees
February 8	0 degrees
February 26	0 degrees
March 19	30 degrees
April 5	30 degrees
May 7	0 degrees
May 31	30 degrees
July 1	30 degrees
August 21	30 degrees
September 2	45 degrees
September 17	60 degrees
November 1	60 degrees
December 3	60 degrees
December 31	90 degrees

2014 Mercury-Mars Aspects

2014 Date	Aspect
January 24	120 degrees
February 16	120 degrees
March 14	120 degrees
April 16	180 degrees
May 12	120 degrees
August 2	90 degrees
August 25	60 degrees
September 11	45 degrees
October 7	45 degrees
October 16	60 degrees
November 21	60 degrees
December 10	45 degrees
December 28	30 degrees

Appendix E

2013 Venus-Mars Aspects

2013 Date	Aspect
February 2	30 degrees
April 7	0 degrees
June 6	30 degrees
July 5	45 degrees
August 2	60 degrees
September 28	90 degrees

2014 Venus-Mars Aspects

2014 Date	Aspect
January 16	90 degrees
March 2	90 degrees
March 29	120 degrees
May 11	180 degrees
July 13	120 degrees
August 27	90 degrees
October 20	60 degrees
November 18	45 degrees
December 19	30 degrees

2013 Mars 90 degrees to Moon

2013 Date	2013 Date
January 6	June 28
January 20	July 14
February 4	July 27
February 18	August 11
March 5	September 9
April 3	September 23
April 18	October 8
May 2	October 21
May 17	November 5
May 30	November 19
June 15	December 4
	December 18

2014 Mars 90 degrees to Moon

2014 Date	2014 Date
January 1	June 28
January 15	July 12
January 29	July 26
February 12	August 9
February 26	August 24
March 11	September 7
March 25	September 21
April 7	October 6
April 20	October 20
May 4	November 4
May 17	November 19

Appendix F

First Trade Dates

TSX 60 Stocks

Stock	Ticker Symbol	First Trade Date
Agnico-Eagle Mines Ltd.	AEM	December 27,1957
Agrium Inc.	AGU	April 20, 1993
ARC Resources Ltd.	ARX	July 10, 1996
Bank of Montreal	BMO	June 9, 1922
Bank of Nova Scotia	BNS	May 16, 1919
Barrick Gold Corporation	ABX	May 2, 1983
BCE Inc.	BCE	July 11, 1905
Bombardier Inc.	BBD/b	September 28, 1976
Brookfield Asset Management	BAM/a	May 19, 1971
Cameco Corporation	CCO	July 4,1991
Canadian Imperial Bank Of Commerce	CM	June 2, 1961
Canadian Natural Resources Limited	CNQ	May 14, 1976
Canadian National Railway Company	CNR	November 17, 1995
Canadian Oil Sands Limited	COS	November 29, 1995
Canadian Pacific Railway Limited	CP	August 21, 2001
Canadian Tire Corporation	CTC/a	January 2, 1945
Crescent Point Energy Corp.	CPG	September 30, 2002
Cenovus Energy Inc.	CVE	November 2, 2009
Eldorado Gold Corporation	ELD	October 22, 1993
Encana Corporation	ECA	August 21, 2001
Enbridge Inc.	ENB	February 15, 1953
Enerplus Corporation	ERF	March 11, 1987
First Quantum Minerals Ltd.	FM	January 11, 2000

Stock	Ticker Symbol	First Trade Date
Fortis Inc.	FTS	November 19, 1969
Gildan Activewear Inc.	GIL	June 18, 1998
Goldcorp Inc.	G	June 20, 1983
Husky Energy Inc.	HSE	October 19, 1993
IAMGOLD Corporation	IMG	March 7, 1986
Imperial Oil Limited	IMO	November 25, 1921
Kinross Gold Corporation	K	July 26, 1983
Loblaw Companies Limited	L	March 13, 1956
Magna International Inc.	MG	December 20, 1962
Manulife Financial Corporation	MFC	December 6, 2001
Metro Inc.	MRU	January 19, 1993
National Bank of Canada	NA	November 1, 1979
Nexen Inc.	NXY	July 14, 1971
Penn West Petroleum Ltd.	PWT	August 1, 1980
Potash Corporation	POT	November 2, 1989
Power Corporation	POW	March 2, 1936
Rogers Communications	RCI/b	April 1, 1971
Research In Motion	RIM	October 21, 1997
Royal Bank of Canada	RY	July 2, 1918
Saputo Inc.	SAP	October 6, 1997
Shoppers Drug Mart	SC	November 20, 2001
Shaw Communications	SJR/b	March 25, 1983
SNC-Lavalin Group Inc	SNC	October 10, 1986
Silver Wheaton Corp.	SLW	October 22, 2004
Sun Life Financial Inc.	SLF	March 23, 2000
Suncor Energy Inc.	SU	September 4, 1979

Stock	Ticker Symbol	First Trade Date
Teck Resources Limited	TCK/b	March 25, 1952
Talisman Energy Inc.	TLM	December 28, 1971
Thomson Reuters Corporation	TRI	March 13, 1980
Tim Hortons Inc.	THI	March 24, 2006
Toronto-Dominion Bank	TD	February 2, 1955
TransAlta Corporation	TA	November 24, 1953
TELUS Corporation	T	January 25, 1999
TransCanada Corporation	TRP	January 2, 1958
Valeant Pharmaceuticals	VRX	June 29, 1987
George Weston Limited	WN	April 19, 1929
Yamana Gold Inc.	YRI	February 9, 1995

Dow Jones Industrial Average Stocks

Stock	Ticker Symbol	First Trade Date
3M	MMM	January 14, 1946
Alcoa	AA	June 11, 1951
American Express	AXP	May 18, 1977
A&T	T	February 15, 1984
Bank of America	BAC	June 28, 1976
Boeing	BA	September 4, 1935
Caterpillar	CAT	December 2, 1929
Chevron	CVX	June 24, 1961
Cisco Systems	CSCO	February 16, 1990
duPont	DD	May 25, 1922
Exxon Mobil	XOM	March 25, 1920
General Electric	GE	May 27, 1926
Hewlett Packard	HPQ	March 17, 1961
Home Depot	HD	September 22, 1981
Intel	INTC	August 7, 1981
IBM	IBM	February 14, 1924
Johnson & Johnson	JNJ	September 25, 1944
JP Morgan	JPM	April 1, 1969
McDonald's	MCD	July 5, 1966
Merck	MRK	May 15, 1946
Microsoft	MSFT	March 13, 1986
Pfizer	PFE	January 17, 1944
Proctor & Gamble	PG	September 12, 1929

Stock	Ticker Symbol	First Trade Date
Coca Cola	KO	September 26, 1944
Travellers Company	TRV	May 11, 1988
United Technologies	UTX	September 5, 1934
United Health Group	UNH	October 17, 1984
Verizon Communications	VZ	July 3, 2000
Wal Mart Stores	WMT	August 25, 1972
Walt Disney	DIS	November 12, 1957

Glossary of Terms

Apogee: Because of the Moon's slightly elliptical pattern of rotation around the Earth, there will be times when it is far from Earth and there will be times when it is close to Earth. The time when the Moon is farthest from Earth is called *apogee*.

Asc: see Ascendant.

Ascendant: One of four cardinal points on a horoscope, the Ascendant is situated in the East.

Aspect: The angular relationship between two planets measured in degrees.

Conjunct: An angular relationship of 0 degrees between two planets.

Descendant: One of four cardinal points on a horoscope, the Descendant is situated in the West.

Detriment: That point within a zodiac sign when a planet is deemed to exhibit unpredictable behaviour.

Direct motion: The normal forward motion of a planet through the zodiac signs when viewed from a vantage point on Earth.

Dsc: see Descendant.

Ecliptic: A planar feature inclined to the Earth's equator at an angle of just over 23 degrees. The various planets and other asteroid bodies rotate around the Sun confined to either side of the ecliptic plane.

Ephemeris: A daily tabular compilation of planetary and lunar positions.

Equinox: An event occurring twice annually, an equinox event marks the time when the tilt of the Earth's axis is neither toward or away from the Sun.

Exaltation: That point within a zodiac sign when a planet is deemed to exhibit powerful influence.

Fall: That point within a zodiac sign when a planet is deemed to exhibit weak influence.

First Trade chart: A zodiac chart depicting the positions of the planets at the time a company's stock or a commodity future commenced trading on a recognized financial exchange.

Full Moon: From a vantage point situated on Earth, when the Moon is seen to be 180 degrees to the Sun.

Geocentric Astrology: That version of astrology in which the vantage point for determining planetary aspects is the Earth.

Heliocentric Astrology: That version of astrology in which the vantage point for determining planetary aspects is the Sun.

IC: see Immum Coeli.

Immum Coeli: One of four cardinal points on a horoscope, the Immum Coeli is situated in the North.

Lunar Eclipse: A lunar eclipse occurs when the Sun, Earth, and Moon are aligned exactly, or very closely so, with the Earth in the middle. The Earth blocks the Sun's rays from striking the Moon.

MC: see Mid-Heaven.

Mid-Heaven: One of four cardinal points on a horoscope, the Mid-Heaven is situated in the South.

New Moon: From a vantage point situated on Earth, when the Moon is seen to be 0 degrees to the Sun.

North Node of Moon: The intersection points between the Moon's plane and Earth's ecliptic are termed the North and South nodes. Astrologers tend to focus on the North node and ephemeris tables clearly list the zodiacal position of the North Node for each calendar day.

Opposition: An angular relationship of 180 degrees between two planets.

Orb: The amount of flexibility or tolerance given to an aspect.

Perigee: Because of the Moon's slightly elliptical pattern of rotation around the Earth, there will be times when it is far from Earth and there will be times when it is close to Earth The time when the Moon is closest to Earth is called *perigee*.

Retrograde motion: The apparent backwards motion of a planet through the zodiac signs when viewed from a vantage point on Earth.

Semi-Sextile: An angular relationship of 30 degrees between two planets.

Semi-Square: An angular relationship of 45 degrees between two planets.

Sextile: An angular relationship of 60 degrees between two planets.

Sidereal Month: The Moon orbits Earth with a slightly elliptical pattern in approximately 27.3 days, relative to a fixed frame of reference.

Sidereal Orbital Period: The time required for a planet to make one full orbit of the Sun as viewed from a fixed vantage point on the Sun.

Solar Eclipse: A solar eclipse occurs when the Moon passes between the Sun and Earth and fully or partially blocks the Sun.

Solstice: An event occurring twice annually, a solstice event marks the time when the Sun reaches its highest or lowest altitude above the horizon at noon.

Square: An angular relationship of 90 degrees between two planets.

Synodic Month: During one sidereal month, Earth has also revolved part way around the Sun, making the average apparent time between one New Moon and the next New Moon longer than the sidereal month at approximately 29.5 days. Also called a lunar month.

Synodic Orbital Period: The time required for a planet to make one full orbit of the Sun as viewed from a fixed vantage point on Earth.

Trine: An angular relationship of 120 degrees between two planets.

Zodiac: an imaginary encircling the 360 degrees of the planetary system divided into twelve equal portions of 30 degrees each.

End Notes

Introduction

1. Stowe, Robinson, Pinto, McLeavey, *Analysis of Equity Investments: Valuation*, AIMR, 2002
2. *Financial Times*, "The Real World MBA FT Report", 2012
3. Jensen, L.J. *AstroCycles and Speculative Markets*, Lambert-Gann Publishing, USA 1978
4. Libra, C. *Astrology-Its Techniques and Ethics*, P. Dz. Veen, Netherlands, 1917
5. Orell, David, *Truth or Beauty*, Oxford University Press, 2012
6. Orell, David, *Economyths*, Ikon Books Ltd (UK), 2012

Chapter 1

1. T. Barton, *Ancient Astrology*, Routledge Publishing, USA, 1994, pp1-113
2. T.W. Griffon, *The Illustrated Guide to Astrology*, Bison Books Ltd, London, 1990, pp 9-90
3. M.Orr, *The Astrological History of the World*, Vega Publishing, London, 2002, pp 1-266
4. R. Hand, *Horoscope Symbols*, Whitford Press, USA, 1981, pp47-79, pp169-179
5. M. Jensen, *Everybody's Astrology*, Libra Cabin, USA, 1922, pp17-22
6. G. Stathis, *Business Astrology 101*, Starcycles Publishing, USA, 2001, pp129-147
7. J&D Parker, *KISS Guide to Astrology*, Dorling Kindersley Publishing, USA, 2000
8. Libra, C. *Astrology-Its Techniques and Ethics*, P. Dz. Veen, Netherlands, 1917 pp 1-52
9. Figure 1-1 Credit—University of Metaphysical Sciences (www.ucmeta.org)

Chapter 2

1. L. MacNeice, *Astrology*, Doubleday & Co., New York, 1964, pp46-50
2. G. Stathis, *Business Astrology 101*, Star Cycles Publishing, USA, 2001, pp 171-172
3. K. Ring, *The Lunar Code*, Random House Publishing, New Zealand, 2006
4. *The Old Farmer's Almanac*, Yankee Publishing, USA, 2012
5. D. Rudhyar, "How to Interpret the Lunar Nodes", *Horoscope Magazine*, June 1966

Chapter 3

1. G. Stathis, *Business Astrology 101*, Starcycles Publishing, USA, 2001, pp129-147
2. H. Weingarten, *Investing by the Stars*, Traders Press Inc, USA, 1996, pp. 65-105
3. www.livephysics.com
4. E. McCaffery, *The Astrological Home Study Course*, Macoy Publishing, USA, 1931.

Chapter 4

1. J. Long *The Universal Clock*, P.A.S. Publications, USA 1978
2. J. Long *Basic Astrotech*, P.A.S. Publications, USA 1989
3. L. Pesavento, *Astro Cycles*, Traders Press, 1983

About The Author

Malcolm Bucholtz, B.Sc., MBA is a graduate of Queen's University Faculty of Engineering in Canada and Heriot Watt University in Scotland where he received an MBA degree. After working in Canadian industry for far too many years, Malcolm followed his passion for the financial markets by becoming an Investment Advisor/Commodity Trading Advisor with an independent brokerage firm in western Canada. Today, he resides in western Canada where he consults to small cap resource companies and trades the financial markets using technical chart analysis, esoteric mathematics and the astrological principles outlined in this book. He maintains both a website (www.investingsuccess.ca) and a blog (www.astrologicaltrading.wordpress.com) where he provides traders and investors with astrological insights into the financial markets.

Index